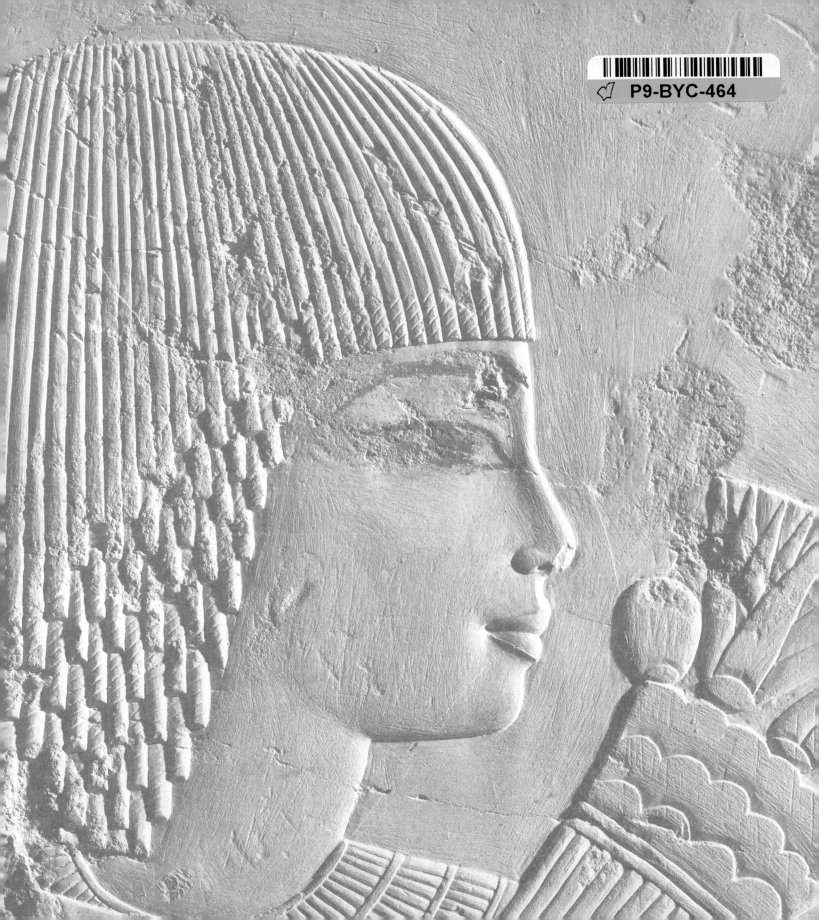

EGYPT

HISTORY AND TREASURES OF AN ANCIENT CIVILIZATION

Giorgio Ferrero

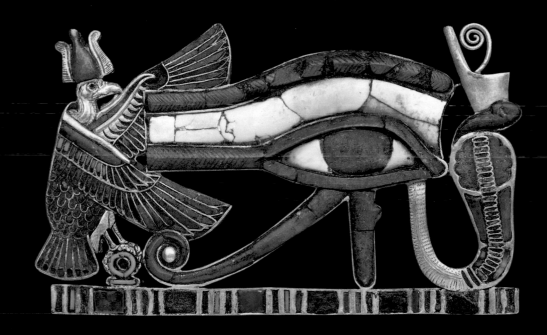

METRO BOOKS

New York

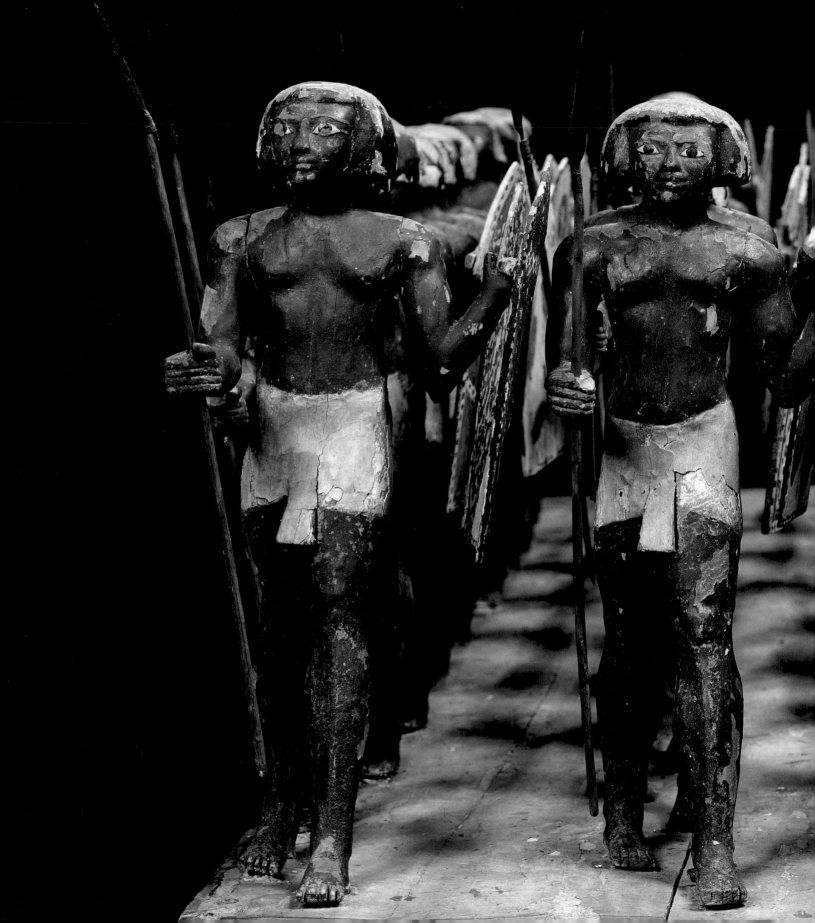

CONTENTS

TEXTS
GIORGIO FERRERO

EDITORIAL DIRECTOR
VALERIA MANFERTO DE FABIANIS

COLLABORATING EDITORS
LAURA ACCOMAZZO
GIORGIO FERRERO

GRAPHIC DESIGNER
PAOLA PIACCO

TRANSLATION
RICHARD PIERCE

METRO BOOKS
New York

An Imprint of Sterling Publishing
387 Park Avenue South
New York, NY 10016

METRO BOOKS and the distinctive Metro Books logo are
trademarks of Sterling Publishing Co., Inc.

© 2010 by White Star Publishers
a registered trademark property of De Agostini Libri S.p.A.

ISBN 978-1-4351-5289-2

For information about custom editions, special sales, and premium
and corporate purchases, please contact Sterling Special Sales
at 800-805-5489 or specialsales@sterlingpublishing.com.

Manufactured in China

2 4 6 8 10 9 7 5 3 1

www.sterlingpublishing.com

1 - TUTANKHAMUN'S INLAID GOLD PENDANT (H. 2 1/4
IN, 5.7 CM) REPRESENTS AN UDJAT EYE (EGYPTIAN
MUSEUM, CAIRO).

2-3 - THE EYES IN TUTANKHAMUN'S GOLDEN MASK
(H. 21 1/4 IN, 54 CM) ARE BORDERED BY LAPIS
LAZULI (EGYPTIAN MUSEUM, CAIRO).

4-5 - QUEEN NEFERTARI MAKING AN OFFERING TO
THE GODDESSES HATHOR, SELKET AND MA'AT IN THIS
PAINTING IN HER TOMB IN THE VALLEY OF THE QUEENS.

6-7 - A WOODEN MODEL (H. 23 1/4 IN, 59 CM)
DEPICTING 40 EGYPTIAN LANCERS FOUND IN A TOMB
AT ASSYUT (EGYPTIAN MUSEUM, CAIRO).

8 - THE FALCON-GOD HORUS PROTECTS KHEPHREN
(H. 5 FT 6 IN, 168 CM; EGYPTIAN MUSEUM, CAIRO).

INTRODUCTION

The magnificent monuments built in ancient Egypt are known around the world, as are the names of the most famous pharaohs in the long history of Egyptian civilization: Khufu, Tutankhamun and Ramesses II. Publications, documentaries, magazines and films continue to dwell on the theme of ancient Egypt, a sign of continuing interest in the story of this great culture. But it was only in 1822, when the intuition of the French scholar Jean-François Champollion paved the way for the first decipherment of hieroglyphs, that the thousands of inscriptions on the ancient Egyptian monuments, steles, statues and tombs could once again bear witness to the life, beliefs and political and economic events of this ancient population that had lived along the banks of the Nile and had created the longest-lived civilization in the history of humanity. With Champollion, modern Egyptology was born, and along with it archaeological research in Egypt, which aimed at finding, preserving and studying the monuments of the pharaohs. This was the motivation behind the 1828 French-Tuscan expedition to Egypt and Nubia headed by Champollion himself and by his Italian disciple Ippolito Rosellini. The "rediscovery" of Egypt and the awareness of and interest in its ancient civilization actually began a few centuries earlier, during the period of Humanism and the Renaissance. The discovery of the Greek text of the Neo-Platonic philosopher Horapollo (4th century AD) concerning hieroglyphic script, *Hieroglyphica*, which was published by Aldo Manuzio in Venice in 1505, marked the beginning of European curiosity concerning ancient Egyptian writing. Another indication of this interest is the art of the time: for example, the woodcuts that illustrated *Hypnerotomachia Poliphili*, an esoteric

Renaissance novel that may have been written by Francesco Colonna, or the paintings by Pinturicchio that decorate the vault of the Sala dei Santi in the Borgia Apartment in the Vatican, depicting the story of Isis and Osiris. For that matter, in Rome during the Renaissance, the popes placed some ancient Egyptian obelisks in the new city squares as part of their efforts to beautify the urban landscape. And in 1527 the humanist intellectual Pietro Bembo purchased the so-called *Mensa Isiaca* (Isiac Table), a bronze tablet of ancient Roman origin with illustrations of Egyptian divinities that is now in the Egyptian Museum, Turin.

In the 17th century, Egyptian mummies and other objects began to arrive in Europe, becoming part of the first antiquarian collections and also contributing to the growing taste for Egyptian forms and motifs, an interest that was encouraged by the publications of the Jesuit Athanasius Kircher regarding the Egyptian monuments in Rome. In the following century European travelers explored the course of the Nile River and "discovered" important monuments, such as the tomb of Ramesses III, which James Bruce visited in 1768. This was a century marked by great attraction for Egypt and Egyptian objects. In fact, what might be called an Egypt-mania spread throughout Europe: Egyptian motifs appeared on furniture and furnishings, such as vases, tea services and clocks, and were used by the Italian architect and engraver Giovanni Battista Piranesi as decorative elements in his famous architectural plates. Mozart's great opera *The Magic Flute*, with the libretto by Emmanuel Schikaneder, was premiered in 1791; its setting was an imaginary ancient Egypt.

10 - THIS GILDED WOOD FLABELLUM (H. 49 1/4 IN, 125 CM) FOUND IN TUTANKHAMUN'S TOMB HAS VITREOUS PASTE INLAY REPRESENTING THE CARTOUCHES OF THE PHARAOH WHICH ARE PROTECTED BY TWO VULTURES (EGYPTIAN MUSEUM, CAIRO).

11 - THIS DETAIL OF THE FACE OF RAMESSES II COMES FROM ONE OF THE COLOSSAL GRANITE STATUES IN THE FIRST COURTYARD OF THE LUXOR TEMPLE THAT PORTRAY THIS FAMOUS 19TH-DYNASTY PHARAOH.

But it was only after Napoleon's military expedition in Egypt in 1798–99 that a truly scientific interest in the archaeology of Egyptian civilization was born, partly stimulated by the publication of Description de l'Égypte, an encyclopedic work containing the observations, studies, finds and drawings of the group of experts and scientists (known as the Savants) who accompanied the French army.

In the early 1800s there were adventurers and travelers such as Giovanni Battista Belzoni and Johann Ludwig Burckhardt whose exploits aroused people's curiosity and imagination concerning the history of ancient Egypt – with the discovery of the tombs of Sethos I, the burial chamber in the pyramid of Khepren, and the Abu Simbel temple. However, it was the second half of the century that witnessed the onset of truly scientific excavations and research: the foundation of the first Egyptian Museum in Cairo (the Bulaq Museum) and the creation of the Egyptian Antiquities Service by the Frenchman Auguste Mariette marked a drastic change in perspective. Interest in ancient Egypt developed alongside the increase in archaeological research. The grandiose monuments along the Nile were depicted in splendid watercolors by the Scottish painter David Roberts, and Mariette himself inspired the libretto for the opera Aida, which Giuseppe Verdi composed on the occasion of the inauguration of the Suez Canal (1871).

Since the late 19th century there has been an uninterrupted series of archaeological discoveries that have greatly increased our knowledge of the history and customs of this great civilization. And certain finds in particular have had a major impact on the history of Egyptology as well as on the public at large. Among these, mention should be made of the discoveries, by Gaston Maspero (1881) and Victor Loret (1898), of the two Theban caches that contained most of the New Kingdom royal mummies; the opening of the tomb of Nefertari in the Valley of the Queens carried out by Ernesto Schiaparelli (1904); and the large hoard of statues found by Georges Legrain in 1903 in the court opposite Pylon VII of the temple of Karnak. But there is no doubt that the most famous and sensational event in this regard was the tomb of the pharaoh Tutankhamun, which Howard Carter found almost intact in 1922. This exceptional discovery triggered a new wave of enthusiasm about Egypt that spread across Europe and the United States: the Art Deco style of architecture and decoration of luxury items in the 1920s and 1930s was greatly influenced by ancient Egyptian forms and iconography. Again in the 1930s, Pierre Montet brought to light the tombs of the Third Intermediate Period pharaohs at Tanis, along with their splendid treasures, marking a new and important stage in Egyptological research. Two other events that struck the international public were the discovery of the funerary barks of Khufu in the Great Pyramid of Giza and the salvage operations of the Nubian temples organized by UNESCO in the 1960s. Many 20th-century and contemporary artists were inspired and continue to be inspired by the iconographic motifs of Egyptian art. Perhaps the most emblematic example of how much the legacy of ancient Egypt has affected the modern world is the decision made by the architect Ieoh Ming Pei to build a glass pyramid as a cover for the large entrance to the Louvre in Paris.

Archaeological research is still underway and, thanks to state-of-the-art techniques and technology, Egyptologists can clarify new aspects of the history of this great civilization. A civilization that never ceases to amaze scholars, enthusiasts and the general public by providing us with exceptional treasures, such as the recently discovered tomb of Ramesses II's children (1989) in the Valley of the Golden Mummies in the Bahariya Oasis (1999), and the 18th-Dynasty tomb found in the Valley of the Kings in 2006.

13 - A PECTORAL (H. 5 3/4 IN, 14.9 CM), WHICH WAS PART OF TUTANKHAMUN'S TREASURE, WITH A SCARAB BEETLE MADE OF SILICA GLASS, A RARE MATERIAL FROM THE LIBYAN DESERT (EGYPTIAN MUSEUM, CAIRO).

CHRONOLOGY

THE BEGINNING
(300,000–3000 BC)

The Nile River Valley is settled by prehistoric communities that adapt to life in this river environment. In the 5th Millennium BC the first Neolithic cultures make their appearance. The Naqada (or Predynastic) culture spreads northward; this process ends around 3000 BC with the unification of Egypt under the rule of the Abydos kings.

THE OLD KINGDOM
(2920–2152 BC)

After the first two dynasties, still part of a formative (Protodynastic) stage, Memphis becomes the capital of Egypt. Djoser, a 3rd-Dynasty pharaoh, builds his funerary complex at Saqqara, including the famous Step Pyramid. The 4th-Dynasty pharaohs Khufu, Khephren and Menkaure' build the pyramids of Giza and the Sphinx, around which lie the necropolises of the royal family and the high-ranking state officials. The 5th Dynasty witnesses the rise of the cult of the sun god Re', to whom the pharaohs dedicate some temples at Abusir. In the 6th Dynasty the pharaohs are buried at Saqqara, Egypt extends its dominion over Nubia, and the power of the provincial governors increases.

THE MIDDLE KINGDOM
(2065–1781 BC)

After a period of political fragmentation (First Intermediate Period), the Theban king Mentuhotpe II again unites Egypt. He builds a mortuary temple at Thebes in the locality of Deir el-Bahri. The 12th-Dynasty kings engage in military expansion in Nubia and begin a reclamation program in the Faiyum region. The 12th-Dynasty pyramids draw inspiration from those built in the Old Kingdom. In the meantime, many provincial necropolises are laid out, and the local governors build large, lavishly decorated tombs for themselves.

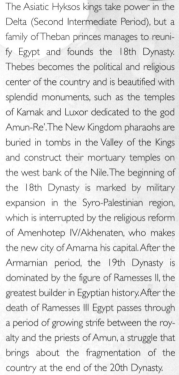

THE NEW KINGDOM
(1550–1075 BC)

The Asiatic Hyksos kings take power in the Delta (Second Intermediate Period), but a family of Theban princes manages to reunify Egypt and founds the 18th Dynasty. Thebes becomes the political and religious center of the country and is beautified with splendid monuments, such as the temples of Karnak and Luxor dedicated to the god Amun-Re'. The New Kingdom pharaohs are buried in tombs in the Valley of the Kings and construct their mortuary temples on the west bank of the Nile. The beginning of the 18th Dynasty is marked by military expansion in the Syro-Palestinian region, which is interrupted by the religious reform of Amenhotep IV/Akhenaten, who makes the new city of Amarna his capital. After the Armarnian period, the 19th Dynasty is dominated by the figure of Ramesses II, the greatest builder in Egyptian history. After the death of Ramesses III Egypt passes through a period of growing strife between the royalty and the priests of Amun, a struggle that brings about the fragmentation of the country at the end of the 20th Dynasty.

THE LATE PERIOD AND FOREIGN DOMINION
(1075–394 BC)

Egypt is split into small principalities and loses its place as an international power. In the mid-8th century BC the Nubian rulers of the 25th Dynasty take power, but after the Assyrian invasion they are replaced by the 26th Dynasty of Sais. In 525 BC the Persians conquer Egypt and turn it into a satrap of the Achaemenid Empire. Egypt regains its independence in 404 BC, but is later subject again to Persian dominion and is conquered by Alexander the Great in 332 BC. Under the Hellenistic sovereigns and the Roman emperors local traditions merge with Greco-Roman elements and beliefs. With the rise of Christianity in the 4th century AD, the civilization of the pharaohs comes to an end.

S A H A R A

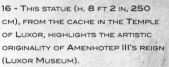

16 - This statue (h. 8 ft 2 in, 250 cm), from the cache in the Temple of Luxor, highlights the artistic originality of Amenhotep III's reign (Luxor Museum).

17 - A fragment of a statue of Queen Teye (h. 2 3/4 in, 7.2 cm) found at Serabit el-Khadim, Sinai (Egyptian Museum, Cairo).

18-19 - The burial chamber in the tomb of Amenhotep II in the Valley of the Kings is supported by six pillars whose surfaces are decorated with illustrations of the pharaoh together with various divinities.

20-21 - The Step Pyramid of Djoser, which dominates the necropolis of Saqqara, represents the first stage in the development of the pyramid; the pyramids of Dahshur, visible in the background, marked the following stage.

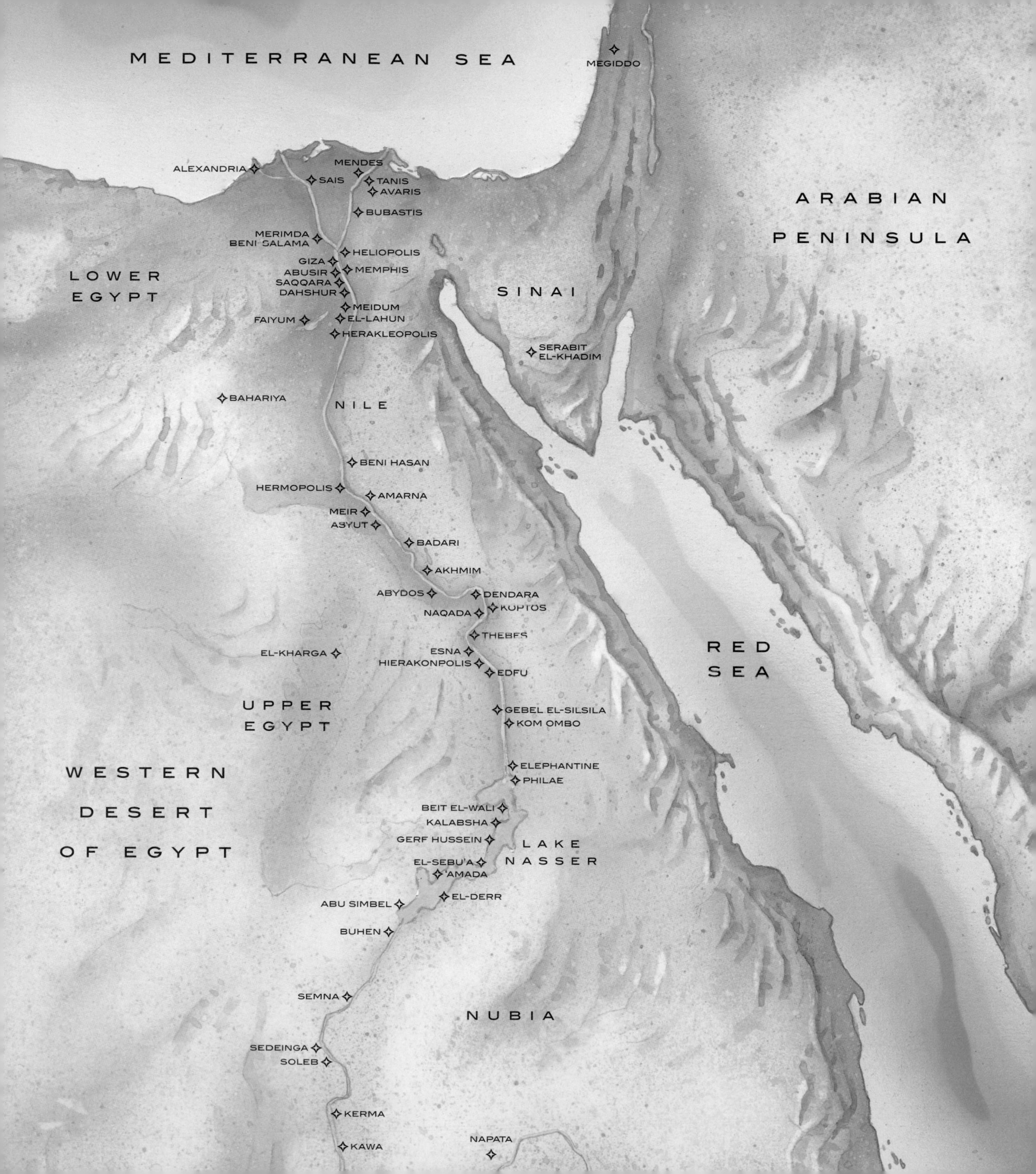

MEDITERRANEAN SEA

MEGIDDO ✧

ARABIAN
PENINSULA

ALEXANDRIA ✧

MENDES
✧ SAIS   ✧
            ✧ TANIS
            ✧ AVARIS

✧ BUBASTIS

LOWER
EGYPT

MERIMDA
BENI-SALAMA
            ✧ HELIOPOLIS
GIZA ✧
ABUSIR   ✧ MEMPHIS
SAQQARA ✧
DAHSHUR ✧
            ✧ MEIDUM
FAIYUM ✧   ✧ EL-LAHUN
            ✧ HERAKLEOPOLIS

SINAI

SERABIT
EL-KHADIM ✧

✧ BAHARIYA

NILE

✧ BENI HASAN

HERMOPOLIS ✧
            ✧ AMARNA
MEIR ✧
ASYUT ✧
            ✧ BADARI

            ✧ AKHMIM

ABYDOS ✧   ✧ DENDARA
NAQADA ✧   ✧ KOPTOS

            ✧ THEBES

EL-KHARGA ✧
            ✧ ESNA
HIERAKONPOLIS ✧
            ✧ EDFU

UPPER
EGYPT

            ✧ GEBEL EL-SILSILA
            ✧ KOM OMBO

RED
SEA

            ✧ ELEPHANTINE
            ✧ PHILAE

WESTERN

DESERT

OF EGYPT

BEIT EL-WALI ✧
KALABSHA ✧
GERF HUSSEIN ✧   LAKE
EL-SEBU'A ✧   NASSER
            ✧ 'AMADA
ABU SIMBEL ✧   ✧ EL-DERR

BUHEN ✧

SEMNA ✧

NUBIA

SEDEINGA ✧
SOLEB ✧

✧ KERMA

✧ KAWA   NAPATA ✧

FROM PREHISTORIC TIMES
TO THE FIRST PHARAOHS

PREHISTORY AND THE NEOLITHIC PERIOD

Human presence in Egypt dates back to the Early Paleolithic period (300,000 years ago), when prehistoric man settled in the depressions and oases of the Western Sahara Desert, around the wells created by climatic conditions that were much more humid than those of the present day. Around 40,000 years ago the climate in North Africa began to change, giving rise to the process of desertification that resulted in the Sahara Desert as we know it today. Due to this change, hunting and fishing communities migrated toward the Nile River, and in the Late Paleolithic (40,000–12,000 years ago) settled along the Nile Valley, where they produced a specialized lithic industry based on small flint tools that was adapted to the new river environment.

The first Neolithic cultures rose up in the Nile Valley around 5200 BC, rather late compared to those of the Near East. The site of Merimda Beni-Salama, about 30 miles (50 km) northwest of Cairo, has yielded the first Egyptian terra-cotta sculptures, which represent human figures and animals. The most outstanding of these is a human head made of clay, the first known representation of an Egyptian face. The Merimda settlement consisted of oval huts, near which large baskets buried in the ground served as granaries where foodstuffs were stored. The graves found in this area bear witness to the custom of burying the deceased lying on one side in a fetal position, often covered with hides or cloth. A more recent Neolithic phase in the Delta area produced the culture of Ma'adi (ca. 3900–3500 BC), a southern suburb of Cairo, where archaeologists brought to light a settlement with varied dwellings: rock-hewn houses, oval huts and rectangular structures. The pottery of the time reveals that there were trade relations with the Palestinian area, while the stone artifacts (schist palettes and mace heads) are a sign that this culture was in contact with the archaeological cultures of Upper Egypt.

Along the Nile Valley, on the other hand, the culture of Badari (ca. 4400–3800 BC), a locality south of Assyut in Middle Egypt, represented the high Neolithic period. The Badarian necropolises, which were made up of oval ditches in which the dead were buried in a contracted position, have yielded a vast range of red pottery with black borders, and smooth pottery with undulations on the surface. Alongside the vessels, other small everyday objects were placed next to the deceased as grave offerings; these included bracelets, beads, ivory and bone combs, rectangular schist palettes and wooden maces. Furthermore, this locality also yielded some terra-cotta and ivory female idols with prominent sexual organs, a hippopotamus carved in ivory, and some clay model boats.

24 LEFT - A NAQADA I PERIOD VASE DECORATED WITH WHITE-COLORED AQUATIC ANIMALS (EGYPTIAN MUSEUM, CAIRO).

24 RIGHT - A NAQADA I PERIOD RED-WARE BOWL (H. 4 1/4 IN, 11 CM) WITH TWO CROCODILES ATTACHED (EGYPTIAN MUSEUM, CAIRO).

23 - DETAIL FROM THE PALETTE OF NA'RMER SHOWING THE FALCON, A ROYAL SYMBOL, GRASPING AN ENEMY WHO, AS SHOWN BY THE PAPYRI, REPRESENTS THE DELTA (EGYPTIAN MUSEUM, CAIRO).

25 LEFT - THIS CLAY HEAD (H. 4 IN, 10.3 CM), FOUND IN THE NEOLITHIC SITE OF MERIMDA BENI-SALAMA , MUST ONCE HAVE HAD HAIR AND A BEARD (EGYPTIAN MUSEUM, CAIRO).

25 RIGHT - A TERRA-COTTA FACE, PERHAPS THE MOST ANCIENT EXAMPLE OF A DEATH MASK, FOUND IN THE PREDYNASTIC NECROPOLIS OF HIERAKONPOLIS (EGYPTIAN MUSEUM, CAIRO).

THE PREDYNASTIC PERIOD

Around 4000 BC, a process began that led to the formation of a dynastic pharaonic state and the birth of Egyptian civilization. The protagonist of this important formative phase, which scholars call the Predynastic period, was the region between Abydos and Luxor. Here, parallel with the final phase of Badarian culture, there developed the Naqada I (or Amratian) culture (ca. 3900–3650 BC), named after the site of the same name situated a few miles north of Luxor. The Naqada I period is famous above all for the finds discovered in many necropolises in this region. A typical product of the Naqada I period is the polished red pottery decorated with creamy white painting. The motifs on the vases range from river fauna to stylized human figures in scenes that can be related to hunting, dances and river navigation. Stone production included stoneware, characterized by its cylindrical shape and support leg, conical club heads, and oval or zoomorphic palettes made of schist.

The following cultural sequence, known as Naqada II or Gerzean (ca. 3650–3300 BC), was initially marked by territorial expansion to the north. The necropolises of the Naqada II period reveal an evolution in the design of tombs, which began to vary in size and shape as well as in the type of grave goods, a sign of progressive social hierarchization. In the field of ceramics production, the pottery was pale pink or grayish, and was decorated with reddish paintings. The most frequently used motifs were geometric patterns or navigation scenes. Boats with curved keels, one or two cabins on the bridge, and prows decorated with animal

horns dominate the scenes of life along the Nile. Human and animal figures were placed in the area around the boats in a rather haphazard manner. The schist palettes become rhomboid in this period, marked by double animal protomes at the ends or relief carving decoration on the surface. Among the terra-cotta representations of human beings, the most famous example is in the Brooklyn Museum of New York: the statuette of a woman with her arms upraised, protruding breasts and bird's head. A particularly fine specimen of the flint knives produced during this age is the one from Gebel el-Arak, now in the Louvre, Paris.

The Naqada II period in Egypt witnessed the rise of the first urban centers, the first examples of which can be identified in the sites of Naqada, Hierakonpolis, el-Kab and Abydos. At Hierakonpolis, excavations brought to light the foundations of what may have been an ancient temple. This site

also yielded one of the most important testaments of Egyptian Predynastic culture – tomb no. 100, a structure that was discovered in the early 1900s and later disappeared. Its painted walls were dominated by six large boats with curved keels and cabins on top, around which were various hunting and war scenes that reflected the iconographic motifs on contemporaneous pottery: entrapped animals, gazelle and chamois hunts and combat scenes. Particularly interesting works were the portrait of a man brandishing two lions (a motif that was also common in Mesopotamian culture) and that of a figure striking three defeated enemies with a club (a motif that would become a classic of pharaonic culture). Boats also dominate the scenes painted on some cloth fragments found in the Predynastic necropolis of Gebelein and now kept in the Egyptian Museum, Turin.

26 LEFT - THIS NAQADA II VASE (H. 4 IN, 22 CM) IS DECORATED WITH A NILOTIC SCENE: A BOAT, A ROW OF OSTRICHES, AND SOME PLANTS (EGYPTIAN MUSEUM, CAIRO)

26 RIGHT - A STONE PALETTE (H. 8 IN, 19 CM) DISCOVERED AT THE SITE OF GERZEH. IT IS DECORATED

WITH A RELIEF OF A COW HEAD AND STARS, WHICH MAY HAVE BEEN AN ARCHAIC REPRESENTATION OF THE GODDESS HATHOR (EGYPTIAN MUSEUM, CAIRO).

27 - VARIOUSLY SHAPED NAQADA I VASES WITH SO-CALLED BLACK-TOPPED DECORATION (EGYPTIAN MUSEUM, CAIRO).

28 AND 29 - THIS SCHIST PALETTE
(H. 12 1/2 IN, 32 CM) DATING FROM THE
LATE NAQADA II PERIOD WAS SCULPTED,
ON THE FRONT SIDE (LEFT), WITH FOUR
DOGS, A BIRD, A LION AND A FANTASTIC
ANIMAL. ON THE BACK (RIGHT) IS THE
SYMMETRICAL MOTIF OF TWO FACING
GIRAFFES SEPARATED BY A PALM TREE
(LOUVRE, PARIS).

"DYNASTY 0" AND THE UNIFICATION OF THE COUNTRY

The development that led to the formation of pharaonic culture and the creation of the ancient Egyptian state reached its climax in the Naqada III period (ca. 3300–3000 BC), whose final phase historians have called "Dynasty 0." Scholars have been engaged in a long-standing debate on the question of how the unification of the pharaonic kingdom and the creation of a single monarchy came about. The ancient Egyptians themselves provided a mythical interpretation of the origin of their history. When the reign of the gods over the Earth ended with the slaying of Osiris and the rise to power of his son Horus, Egypt was presumably ruled by some heroic personages known as the "companions of Horus"; after them, the unification of the nation, divided into two political entities, was realized by King Menes, the founder of the 1st Dynasty. For quite some time it was believed that Na'rmer, a sovereign depicted on a stone palette found at Hierakonpolis, was to be identified with the Menes mentioned in ancient Egyptian sources. The relief images carved on the palette, now kept in the Egyptian Museum of Cairo, represent war and battle scenes that seem to suggest the unification of the kingdom. On one side the king, who is wearing the white crown symbolizing Upper Egypt, is overpowering an enemy from the Delta region. This motif is expressed by means of the representation of a falcon wrapping a rope around the head of an enemy whose body is represented by a papyrus plant (the symbol of Lower Egypt). In the lower register, two enemies are fleeing from a city represented from a bird's-eye view of the walls. On the other side of the palette King Na'rmer, accompanied by two dignitaries and some standard-bearers, is reviewing the enemies' corpses. Another battle scene completes the low-

er register: a bull (the symbol of royalty) is striking an enemy and conquering his city. However, archaeological research seems to indicate that the unification of Egypt was not effected by a single king but rather was the result of a long and slow process of cultural assimilation of Lower Egypt by Upper Egypt.

The representation of this unification process and the struggles it entailed can be seen on the relief carvings that decorate the large number of ceremonial stone palettes dating from the Naqada III period. On the so-called Vultures' Palette, the lion killing an enemy is the symbolic representation of a king celebrating a military victory. Another artifact connected to the unification of the kingdom is the so-called Palette of the Libyan Tribute, on one side of which are cities conquered and destroyed by zoomorphic figures that may represent the names of the same number of kings.

Archaeological digs carried out in the necropolis of Abydos have yielded the tombs of the local rulers from the Naqada III period, who presumably gave rise to the kings of the first dynasty in ancient Egypt. An especially important discovery, made in 1988, was the Tomb U-j, which belonged to a king of the so-called Dynasty 0 known as Scorpion I. This tomb, whose plan is a reproduction of the model of a palace, contained numerous jars used for wine and beer, on whose ivory or bone labels are carved the first known examples of hieroglyphic script (which can be dated at around 3150 BC). Another archaeological document dating from Dynasty 0 pertains to the Predynastic king known as Scorpion II: a stone mace-head found in pieces at Hierakonpolis whose decoration depicts the sovereign digging the first trench with a hoe.

30 - The Palette of the Libyan Tribute (h. 7 1/2 in, 19 cm) has rows of animals and trees (right) as well as zoomorphic figures in the act of destroying some cities (Egyptian Museum, Cairo).

31 - The Palette of Na'rmer (h. 2 ft, 64 cm) represents the victory of the king of Abydos, Na'rmer, against an enemy from the North and also anticipates classic scenes of pharaonic iconography (Egyptian Museum, Cairo).

32-33 - Detail of the Palette of Na'rmer showing the king wearing a red crown preceded by standard-bearers and a court official and followed by the sandal-bearing official (Egyptian Museum, Cairo).

THE AGE OF THE PYRAMIDS:
THE OLD KINGDOM

THE PROTODYNASTIC PERIOD

The period of the first two ancient Egyptian dynasties (2920–2649 BC) is also known as the Protodynastic or "Thinite" Period, after Thinis, the locality near Abydos where the first kings of Egypt came from. The founder of the 1st Dynasty, Menes, most likely corresponds to King 'Aha, who was buried in the Abydos necropolis and was the direct successor of Na'rmer. All the 1st-Dynasty rulers were buried at Abydos in burial chambers surrounded by secondary chambers and storerooms. The tombs were probably covered with tumuli and marked by a pair of steles with the name of the owner, as can be seen in the case of the stele of Queen Mereneith, the mother of the pharaoh Den, and that of the pharaoh Djet, which is in the Louvre, Paris. The tomb of Djer, the pharaoh who succeeded 'Aha, yielded some gold and lapis lazuli bracelets, thus bearing witness to a prosperous period and an Egypt that was already part of a circuit of international trade. Associated with the royal tombs of Abydos were some monumental funerary precincts made of unfired bricks; these were separated from the necropolis, and their walls reproduced those of the archaic royal palaces, with niches and protuberances on the façades. Only the funerary enclosure of Kha'sekhemwy (*Shunet el-Zebib*), the last 2nd-Dynasty pharaoh, has preserved its massive walls, which are over 30 feet high; only the foundations remain of the other ones. In 1991 archaeologists discovered 14 canals for barks that contained the remains of wooden vessels about 75 ft (23 m) long whose presence, linked with the monumental enclosures, suggests that a royal funerary cult was practiced there.

The main written source describing the events of the first Egyptian dynasties is the so-called Palermo Stone, a stele that was probably inscribed during the 5th Dynasty and which narrates the principal events of the individual reigns. The Palermo Stone tells us that 'Aha founded the city of Memphis at the spot where the Nile Valley and Delta meet (this city was the capital of the Egyptian state in the following centuries).

In the Memphis area, or more precisely, in northern Saqqara, archaeologists found an important necropolis with tombs dating back to the 1st and 2nd Dynasties that belonged to high-ranking officials in this zone. Here, along the edge of a rocky escarpment, were built large mastaba tombs, freestanding rectangular structures modeled after the mansions or palaces of the time. Mastaba S 3035, which belonged to Hemaka, an official during the reign of Den, yielded grave goods that included two decorated stone disks, a roll of papyrus on which nothing was written, small vases for cosmetics and some ivory labels.

The first three pharaohs of the 2nd Dynasty (Hetepsekhemwy, Re'neb and Ninetjer, 2770–2649 BC) decided to move their burial site from Abydos to Memphis and were interred in southern Saqqara. The only remains of their tombs are long underground passageways; the superstructures no longer exist. In contrast, the last two pharaohs of this dynasty, Peribsen and Kha'sekhemwy, had themselves buried in the royal necropolis of Abydos. Peribsen was interred in a small tomb, where archaeologists found two steles, which surprisingly bore the name of the pharaoh in association with the figure of the god Seth. The tomb of Kha'sekhemwy, which is of monumental proportions, yielded part of its grave goods; there are also two statues of this pharaoh that represent him seated on his throne wearing official royal festival garb and the white crown of Upper Egypt.

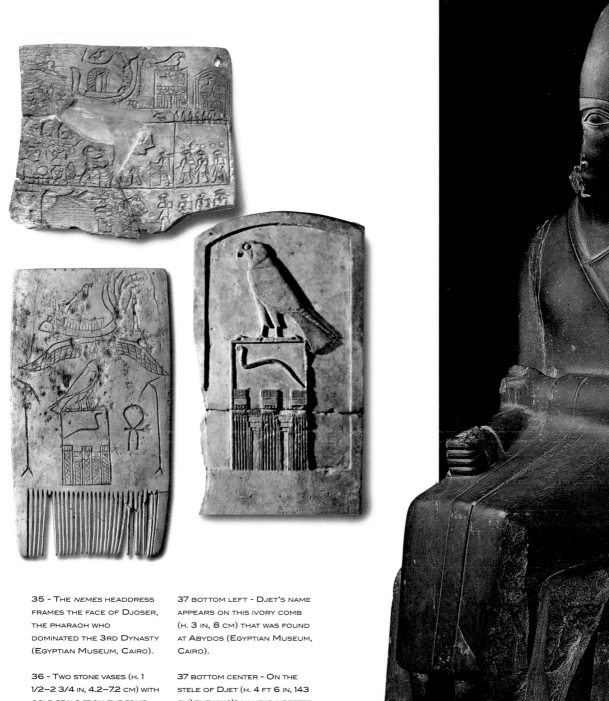

35 - The *nemes* headdress frames the face of Djoser, the pharaoh who dominated the 3rd Dynasty (Egyptian Museum, Cairo).

36 - Two stone vases (h. 1 1/2–2 3/4 in, 4.2–7.2 cm) with gold seals from the tomb of Kha'sekhemwy at Abydos (Egyptian Museum, Cairo).

37 top - An ivory label (h. 1 3/4 in, 4.8 cm) dating from the reign of King 'Aha used to indicate the contents of an amphora (Egyptian Museum, Cairo).

37 bottom left - Djet's name appears on this ivory comb (h. 3 in, 8 cm) that was found at Abydos (Egyptian Museum, Cairo).

37 bottom center - On the stele of Djet (h. 4 ft 6 in, 143 cm) the king's name is inserted in a *serekh* surmounted by a falcon (Louvre, Paris).

37 right - The statue of Kha'sekhemwy seated on his throne (h. 1 ft 10 in, 56 cm) and wearing his jubilee garb comes from Hierakonpolis (Egyptian Museum, Cairo).

38

38 LEFT – A STATUE OF THE ENTHRONED DJOSER (H. 4 FT 6 IN, 142 CM) IN JUBILEE DRESS WAS FOUND IN A CHAPEL (*SERDAB*) IN THE ROYAL FUNERARY COMPLEX AT SAQQARA (EGYPTIAN MUSEUM, CAIRO).

38 RIGHT – HEZYRE', AN OFFICIAL AT DJOSER'S COURT, IS PORTRAYED HERE SEATED AT AN OFFERINGS TABLE, ABOVE WHICH IS THE LIST OF THE GIFTS MADE TO THE DECEASED (EGYPTIAN MUSEUM, CAIRO).

39 – A WOODEN PANEL (H. 3 FT 9 IN, 114 CM) FROM THE MASTABA OF HEZYRE' AT SAQQARA IN WHICH THIS LEADING OFFICIAL IS HOLDING A SCRIBE'S TOOLS, A STAFF AND SCEPTER (EGYPTIAN MUSEUM, CAIRO).

At the beginning of the 3rd Dynasty (2649–2575 BC) the center of public, political and economic life in Egypt shifted definitively to Memphis. This dynasty was dominated by the figure of Djoser (Netjerykhet, 2630–2611 BC), the first pharaoh who built a stone funerary complex and a pyramid. The idea of transforming the mastaba tomb structure into a step pyramid was conceived by Imhotep, a priest from Heliopolis and the pharaoh's chief architect, who was later venerated as a divinity. Another official during the reign of Djoser was Hezyre', who was buried in a mastaba at Saqqara (S 2405), in which archaeologists found wooden panels with portraits of him standing and seated, accompanied by his honorifics.

Sekhemkhet, who was Djoser's successor, began the construction of a funerary complex at Saqqara that was left unfinished, while another step pyramid, probably belonging to the pharaoh Kha'ba, is situated at Zawyet el-'Aryan, north of Saqqara. The last pharaoh of this dynasty, Huni, is most probably to be credited with the construction of some small step pyramids in provincial localities such as Zawyet el-Maiyitin, Abydos, Naqada, el-Kula, Edfu and Elephantine, whose purpose has not yet been clarified.

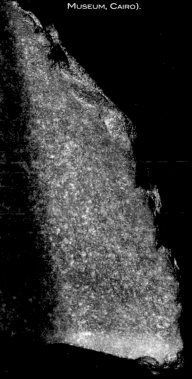

The 4th Dynasty (2575–2465 BC) began under Snofru (2575–2551 BC), the sole pharaoh who is attributed as the builder of three pyramids. The only known likeness of Snofru's son Cheops, or Khufu (2551–2528 BC), who built the Great Pyramid of Giza, is a small statue now kept in the Egyptian Museum, Cairo; his son Djedefre' built his pyramid north of Giza, in the locality of Abu Rawash, where a sphinx's head now in the Louvre was found. Khephren (2520–2494 BC) moved the royal necropolis back to Giza. In his pyramid was found one of the best-known statues in ancient Egyptian art, in which this pharaoh is depicted seated on his throne with the falcon representing the god Horus spreading its wings around the ruler's neck as a sign of protection. There are several portraits of Menkaure', or Mycerinus (2490–2472 BC), the builder of the third pyramid of Giza; he is depicted either alone, together with a consort, or as part of a triad that also includes the goddess Hathor and a provincial goddess. The 4th Dynasty ended with Shepseskaf (2472–2465 BC), who had a large mastaba that looks like a sarcophagus built at southern Saqqara.

Despite the fact that the pyramids of Giza had already been pillaged in ancient times, an exceptional archaeological find was made in 1925 at Giza: 4th-Dynasty royal funerary regalia and furnishings, miraculously spared by grave robbers, were discovered in a funerary shaft that was reused as the tomb of Queen Hetepheres I, the consort of Snofru and mother of Cheops. Among the objects found there were an empty alabaster sarcophagus, the most ancient canopic jars known to us, beds, sedan chairs and wooden thrones dressed with gold leaf, as well as precious boxes and receptacles.

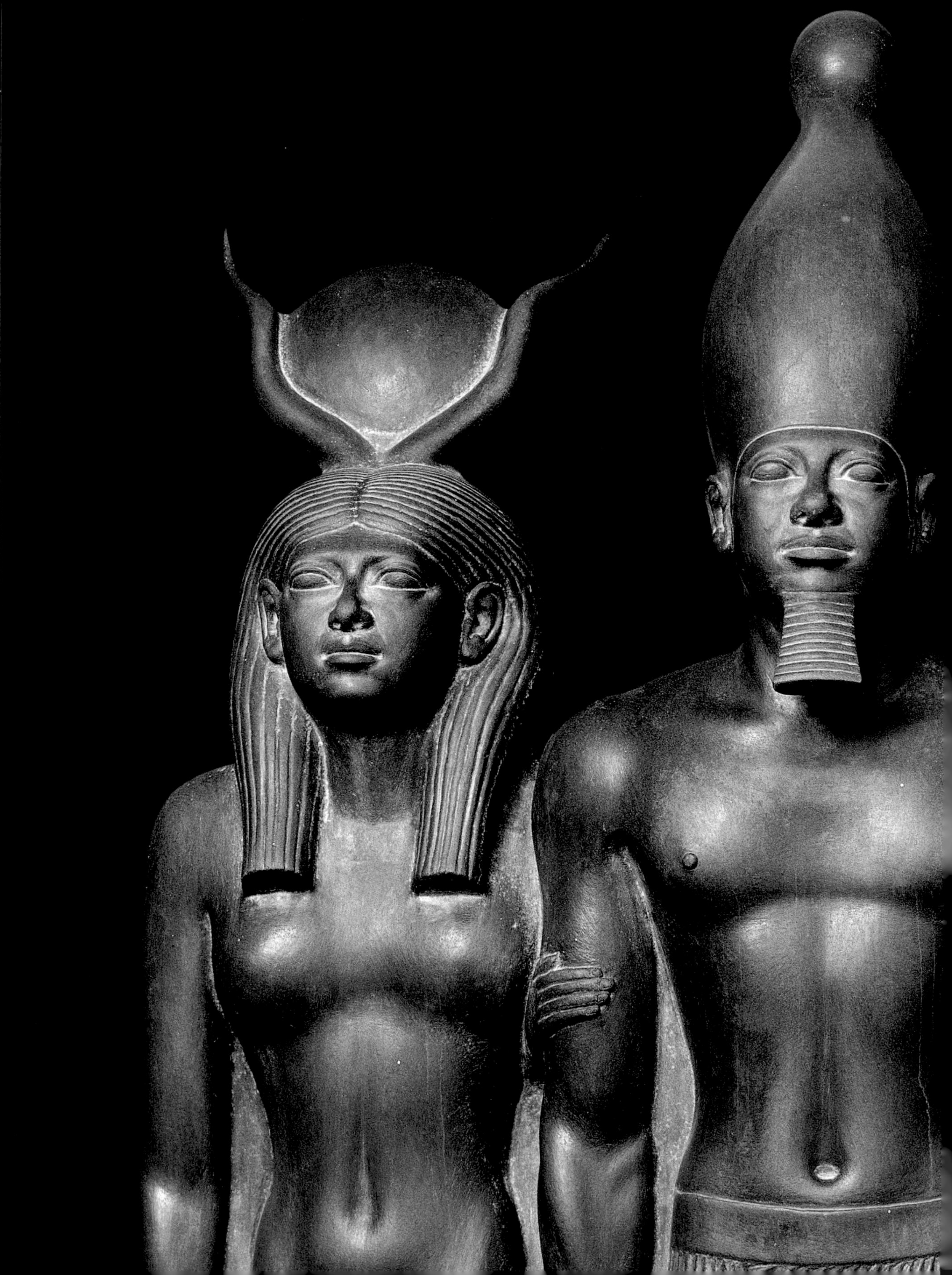

42-43 - MENKAURE' (MYCERINUS), WEARING THE WHITE CROWN OF UPPER EGYPT, IS FLANKED BY THE GODDESS HATHOR (LEFT) AND BY THE TUTELARY DIVINITY OF THE *NOME* OF KINOPOLIS (RIGHT). IN THE PHARAOH'S VALLEY TEMPLE AT GIZA ARCHAEOLOGISTS FOUND FOUR TRIADS LIKE THIS ONE (H. 3 FT, 92.5 CM; EGYPTIAN MUSEUM, CAIRO).

44

44-45 - A WOODEN BED
DRESSED WITH GOLD LEAF (L.
5 FT 10 IN, 178 CM) THAT WAS
AMONG THE GRAVE GOODS OF
QUEEN HETEPHERES I
(EGYPTIAN MUSEUM, CAIRO).

44 CENTER - A RECEPTACLE
(L. 5 FT 2 IN, 157.5 CM) USED
TO CONTAIN THE BALDACHIN
OF QUEEN HETEPHERES I,
WITH INLAY DECORATION
(EGYPTIAN MUSEUM, CAIRO).

44 BOTTOM - THE SILVER
BRACELETS WITH INLAY
BELONGING TO HETEPHERES I
LIE IN A GILDED WOODEN
COFFER (L. 16 1/2 IN, 41.9 CM;
EGYPTIAN MUSEUM, CAIRO).

45 TOP - THIS CHAIR (H. 31 1/4
IN, 79.5 CM) FROM THE TOMB
OF HETEPHERES I AT GIZA
HAS LEGS IN THE SHAPE OF A
LION'S PAWS AND ARMRESTS
THAT LOOK LIKE INTERWOVEN
PAPYRUS STALKS (EGYPTIAN
MUSEUM, CAIRO).

45 BOTTOM LEFT - THESE
BOWLS AND GOLD VASE WERE
FOUND IN 1925 TOGETHER
WITH QUEEN HETEPHERES I'S
GRAVE GOODS (EGYPTIAN
MUSEUM, CAIRO).

45 BOTTOM RIGHT -
HETEPHERES I'S PALANQUIN (H.
20 1/2 IN, 52 CM), FURNISHED
WITH A STAFF, WAS DECORATED
WITH GOLD LEAF. AN
INSCRIPTION ON THE BACK
BEARS THE QUEEN'S TITLES
(EGYPTIAN MUSEUM, CAIRO).

The 5th Dynasty (2465–2323 BC) marked the rise of the cult of the sun god Re', whose religious center was Heliopolis, near Cairo. Userkaf (2465–2458 BC), who chose to be buried in a modest pyramid at the site of northern Saqqara, was the first pharaoh to build a sun temple in honor of the dynastic god Re' at Abusir, a few miles north of Saqqara. This sun temple looked like a platform on which rose up a stone obelisk – a symbol of the sun god linked with the primordial hill (*benben*) that emerged from the waters of chaos – connected to a valley temple by means of a processional causeway. The sun temple built by Neuserre' (2416–2392 BC), the sixth ruler of this dynasty, in the locality of Abu Ghurab, north of Abusir, is well preserved: in front of the base of the obelisk is a large alabaster altar, while at the western end of the terrace there are nine alabaster basins used for sacrifices. The walls of the roofed passageways that once delimited the temple platform were decorated with relief sculpture depicting the various seasons, Egyptian flora and fauna, and the celebration of the pharaoh's jubilee feast. A short distance away from the platform, an imita-

tion of the sun god's bark, made of bricks and wood, completed the complex. The pharaohs Sahure', Neferirkare' Kakai, Ra'neferef and Neuserre' Izi, as well as Queen Khentkaus II (probably the mother of the last two rulers), all built their pyramids at Abusir. The funerary complex of Sahure' yielded some bas-relief sculpture representing the return of the Egyptian naval expeditions from Lebanon and from the distant land of Punt, which may correspond to the present-day Horn of Africa.

In the archives of the funerary complexes of Neferirkare' Kakai and Ra'neferef archaeologists discovered a series of papyri that are the largest and most important source of information regarding the administration and economic life of the Old Kingdom temples. The last two 5th-Dynasty rulers, Djedkare' Izezi (2388–2356 BC) and Wenis (2356–2323 BC), decided to have their tombs built in the necropolis of Saqqara. During the reign of Wenis, the walls of the inner chambers of the pyramid were covered, for the first time, with hieroglyphic inscriptions arranged in vertical columns. These were the *Pyramid Texts*, the most ancient religious literature found in Egypt.

46 - SCULPTURE GROUP (H. 5 FT 9 IN, 64 CM) DEPICTING THE ENTHRONED SAHURE' FLANKED BY THE DIVINITY OF THE *NOME* OF KOPTOS WHO IS OFFERING HIM THE SYMBOL OF LIFE (METROPOLITAN MUSEUM OF ART, NEW YORK).

47 - THIS HIGHLY STYLIZED HEAD (H. 14 1/2 IN, 45 CM), WHICH WAS PART OF A SCHIST STATUE OF KING USERKAF, WAS FOUND AT THE SUN TEMPLE NEAR ABUSIR (EGYPTIAN MUSEUM, CAIRO).

The first pharaoh of the 6th Dynasty (2323–2152 BC), Teti (2323–2291 BC), also had his pyramid constructed at Saqqara. An autobiographical text carved by a court official named Uni in his tomb at Abydos has provided us with information concerning the reigns of the successive pharaohs, Pepy I (2289–2255 BC) and Merenre' I (2255–2246 BC). These two kings, two splendid copper statues of which were found at Hierakonpolis, pursued an expansionist policy to the south with the aim of securing control of the commerce of precious goods that came from Nubia, gold first and foremost. The Egyptian military and trade expeditions carried out during the 6th Dynasty are also in other texts carved in the tombs of the state officials of Elephantine, which were hewn out of the cliff on the western bank of the Nile (Qubbet el-Hawa). In particular, the autobiography of Harkhuf, the governor of Elephantine during the reign of Pepy II (2246–2152 BC), contains an account of three Egyptian expeditions in Nubian territory, south of the Second Cataract.

After Pepy II's long reign, the 6th Dynasty ended with a series of short-lived rulers who were unable to counter the grave crisis of the Egyptian state apparatus. In fact, during the 6th Dynasty the power of the provincial governors and nobles had increased beyond royal control and they had begun to create feudal-type sovereign states, as is attested by the exceptional development and wealth of the provincial necropolises of Akhmim, Abydos, Edfu and Elephantine. Thus, the progressive weakening of the central authority and the growing power of the local principalities led to the collapse of the political system that had sustained Egypt for almost five centuries during the Old Kingdom and that had created the magnificent monuments of the age of the pyramids.

48 - A STOREROOM IN THE TEMPLE OF HORUS AT HIERAKONPOLIS YIELDED THIS COPPER STATUE (H. 25 IN, 177 CM) OF KING PEPY I THAT STILL HAS THE OBSIDIAN AND LIMESTONE USED TO DEPICT THE EYES (EGYPTIAN MUSEUM, CAIRO).

49 - THIS FALCON HEAD MADE OF GOLD (H. 17 3/4 IN, 37.5 CM) PROBABLY DATES FROM THE 6TH DYNASTY AND WAS FOUND IN THE TEMPLE OF HORUS AT HIERAKONPOLIS. THE HEADDRESS WITH A URAEUS AND TWO FEATHERS WAS MADE AT A LATER DATE (EGYPTIAN MUSEUM, CAIRO).

THE GREAT ROYAL NECROPOLISES

The great heritage of the Old Kingdom consists of the funerary complexes in the Memphite area, which include the largest Egyptian pyramids. These grandiose structures were the result of architectural as well as symbolic–religious elaboration that can be traced through the various dynasties. Starting off from the simple square mastaba, Imhotep, King Djoser's architect, erected at Saqqara a six-step pyramid about 200 ft (62 m) high. Underneath the pyramid was a complex network of galleries that served as the pharaoh's mortuary chamber proper, whose corridors were decorated with small faïence tiles. The step pyramid was placed in a large rectangular area, oriented on a north–south axis and bounded by a wall with niches that reproduced the façade of a palace. The entrance of the complex consisted of a long porticoed corridor supported by bundle columns that ended in a hypostyle atrium with eight columns. Perched on

the north façade of the pyramid was the mortuary temple, near which was the ramp that led to the underground chambers. Again on the north side of the pyramid was a small chapel (*serdab*) that contained the statue of the deceased pharaoh, which is now kept in the Egyptian Museum, Cairo. The north court of the pyramid ended with a chapel inserted in the outer wall, where there was a large altar cut out of the stone; the south court of the pyramid housed two slabs that represented the frontiers of Egypt and ended with the so-called South Tomb, an imitation sepulcher that was probably used for the cult of the dead pharaoh and that, in the underground structure, reproduced the network of galleries of the main pyramid. The east side of the complex housed a composite series of stone edifices connected with the celebration of the *Sed*, a royal festival held in the 30th year of the pharaoh's reign. In a small courtyard were two facing rows of chapels preced-

ed by a court that represented the tabernacles of the provincial divinities of Egypt. A pedestal must have been used to support the double throne on which the king, as the ruler of Upper and Lower Egypt, participated in the *Sed* ceremony. Behind the *Sed* festival courtyard was "Temple T," perhaps a royal palace. Completing the east side of the Djoser complex, right next to the step pyramid, are the so-called North and South Pavilions, two edifices that must have been symbolic representations of the sanctuaries of Upper and Lower Egypt.

50 - THE *SED* FESTIVAL COURTYARD IN THE FUNERARY COMPLEX OF DJOSER AT SAQQARA HAS A SET OF STONE CHAPELS THAT REPRODUCE THE FORMS OF THE ARCHAIC WOODEN TABERNACLES.

50-51 - THE FUNERARY COMPLEX OF DJOSER AT SAQQARA IS DOMINATED BY THE FAMOUS SIX-LEVEL STEP PYRAMID, WHICH IS THE FIRST EXAMPLE OF AN EGYPTIAN PYRAMID.

51 - A GRECO-ROMAN BRONZE STATUETTE (H. 8 1/2 IN, 21.5 CM) PORTRAYING IMHOTEP, THE ARCHITECT OF DJOSER, WHO IS HOLDING A PAPYRUS SCROLL AND IS IDENTIFIED AS THE SON OF PTAH (EGYPTIAN MUSEUM, CAIRO).

The transition from the step pyramid to the classical pyramid with smooth, straight sides took place during the reign of the first 4th-Dynasty pharaoh, Snofru. At Maidum, along the edge of the Faiyum oasis, this ruler commissioned the construction of an eight-step pyramid 278 ft (85 m) high, which, near the end of his reign, was dressed in order to obtain a smooth surface. The removal of this casing, which took place in ancient times, revealed the inner structure of the pyramid and the levels of the steps. An important new element in the Maidum complex was the position of the funerary apartments, which were no longer hewn out of earth and were accessible by means of a vertical shaft, but were now included in the body of the pyramid and connected by means of an access corridor that was open on the north façade. On the left side of the Maidum pyramid is a small offerings temple, from which began a processional causeway connected to a valley temple. The symbolic burial site, represented in the Djoser complex by the South Tomb, was transformed here into a small step pyramid again situated on the south side. The second pyramid that Snofru built lies in Dahshur, 30 miles (50 km) north of the preceding one, and is known as the Bent (or Rhomboidal) Pyramid because of the characteristic double "bends" of its façades. The pharaoh had commissioned his architects to build a pyramid 490 ft (150 m) high, but the excessive inclination forced the builders to modify the gradient during construction and finally to abandon the project altogether. The Bent Pyramid has a small chapel-temple with two steles on its east side and a subsidiary pyramid on the south side. The third pyramid built by Snofru, again at Dahshur, is called the Red Pyramid, which is the first structure of this kind to have entirely smooth dressing. This monument is 340 ft (105 m) high and has a less inclined silhouette than the Bent Pyramid. The three mortuary chambers, hewn out of the pyramid on ground level, have a corbelled ceiling, so built in order to relieve the enormous weight the side walls had to support.

52-53 - THE BENT PYRAMID OF DAHSHUR IS CHARACTERIZED BY ITS DOUBLE INCLINATION, PRODUCED BY A CHANGE DURING CONSTRUCTION FROM THE ORIGINAL ARCHITECTURAL PROJECT.

53 - THE STEPPED INTERIOR OF THE PYRAMID OF SNOFRU AT MAIDUM IS VISIBLE TODAY BECAUSE THE SMOOTHED OUTER CASING OF THIS MONUMENT COLLAPSED.

The apogee of Old Kingdom architecture was achieved with the pyramids of Giza. The Great Pyramid of Khufu, which is 479 ft (146 m) high and has a base measuring 754 ft (230 m), still amazes us for its perfect proportions and precise astronomical orientation. The structure of the inner chambers is articulated in a much more complex manner than in the earlier pyramids. An ascending corridor leads to the so-called Great Gallery, a huge hall 154 ft (47 m) long and 27 ft (8.5 m) high supported by a gigantic corbelled ceiling. From here there is access to the burial chamber (the King's Chamber), which contains an empty sarcophagus and over which are five discharge chambers separated by monolithic blocks of granite weighing 40 tons and surmounted by a gabled roof. Some narrow vents lead from the chamber toward the exterior of the pyramid; these were probably symbolic passageways through which the king could get to the circumpolar stars of the firmament, which were connected to Egyptian mortuary beliefs. A horizontal corridor that starts off from the Great Gallery leads to another smaller chamber (the Queen's Chamber), where there is a niche that was probably used to house a statue. The third chamber in the pyramid, which is 98 ft (30 m) underground, was not finished, like a blind corridor that also begins there. The exterior of the pyramid bears traces of five pits for barks, one of which contained a wooden boat that was carefully restored and is now on display in a museum at Giza built expressly to house it. On the east side of the pyramid stood the mortuary temple, whose only trace is a part of the basalt floor; the valley temple, on the other hand, has not yet been investigated by archaeologists because it is buried under the modern suburbs of Cairo. Three small pyramids used as the tombs of three queens lie at the east corner of the Great Pyramid. Recently, archaeologists found traces of the city of the priests who officiated the king's mortuary ceremony to the south of the mortuary temple, in the same area that housed the royal palace, from which the pharaoh could observe the construction of his tomb.

54 - THIS STATUE (H. 5 FT 1 IN, 155.5 CM) OF PRINCE HEMIUNU, WHO CONCEIVED THE GREAT PYRAMID AT GIZA, COMES FROM HIS MASTABA AT THE SAME SITE (ROEMER- UND PELIZAEUS-MUSEUM, HILDESHEIM).

54-55 - THE GREAT PYRAMID OF KHUFU IS FLANKED BY THE NECROPOLISES OF THE OLD KINGDOM NOBLES. ON THE EAST SIDE ARE THE REMAINS OF THE PAVEMENT OF THE MORTUARY TEMPLE AND TWO PITS FOR BARKS.

55 TOP - THE GRAND GALLERY, WHICH IS 154 FT (47 M) LONG, IS THE LARGEST AREA IN KHUFU'S GREAT PYRAMID AT GIZA.

55 BOTTOM - THE WOODEN BOAT
(L. 141 FT, 43 M) DISCOVERED IN 1954
IN ONE OF THE BARK PITS CONNECTED TO
THE GREAT PYRAMID OF KHUFU WAS
RESTORED AND REASSEMBLED. ITS PROW
AND STERN ARE DECORATED WITH
PAPYRUS BUDS.

The Pyramid of Khephren, which is the second largest after the Great Pyramid of Khufu, still has some of its original limestone casing. The interior structure of this pyramid is much simpler and more linear than that of Khufu: two entranceways lead to a descending passage that in turn leads to a subsidiary hall; the burial chamber, on ground level, is large and contains a black granite sarcophagus. For the first time, in the complex of Khephren, a large and articulated mortuary temple was built, including a vast courtyard with pillars and niches used to house the royal statues. The valley temple, access to which was afforded by a processional ramp positioned diagonally, had a T-shaped courtyard with 16 monolithic pillars dressed with red granite that supported long architraves made of the same material.

Next to this sanctuary is one of the most famous and enigmatic ancient Egyptian monuments: the Great Sphinx. This gigantic sculpture, which represents an imaginary being with a human head and lion's body, was carved out of a rocky outcrop in the plain of Giza. It is commonly thought that the Sphinx has the facial features of Khephren, even though a recently formulated hypothesis has it that this was the work of Khufu. A sanctuary, built next to the valley temple of Khephren, was connected to the Sphinx; it had a large central courtyard with a colonnade made up of rectangular pillars.

The pyramid of Menkaure', which is the smallest of the three, was once 213 ft (65 m) high and was partly dressed with red granite. The four inner chambers of this pyramid have a rather complex layout, which may have been due to the changes made in the original project. The mortuary temple had a large porticoed courtyard that was finished by Shepseskaf, while the valley temple was finished with bricks in a later period. The main pyramid is flanked by three secondary ones: two step pyramids and one with smooth faces, in which the queens were buried.

56 - THE PYRAMID OF KHEPHREN STILL
HAS PART OF ITS ORIGINAL CASING.

57 TOP LEFT - INSIDE THE PYRAMID
OF MENKAURE' IS A CHAMBER WITH
SIX NICHES.

57 TOP RIGHT - ONE CHAMBER IN
THE PYRAMID OF MENKAURE' HAS
MOLDING DECORATION.

57 BOTTOM - THE SPHINX OF GIZA,
THE VERY SYMBOL OF PHARAONIC
EGYPT, STANDS OUT IN THE GIZA PLAIN
NEAR KHEPHREN'S VALLEY TEMPLE.

58-59 - THE PYRAMIDS OF KHUFU,
KHEPHREN AND MENKAURE', WHICH
DOMINATE THE GIZA PLAIN, MARK THE
APOGEE OF OLD KINGDOM ROYAL
FUNERARY ARCHITECTURE.

The transition to the 5th Dynasty marked a change in the building technique of the funerary monuments. The pyramids at Abusir are a great deal smaller than those at Giza, but within the context of the mortuary complex taken as a whole they were planned in a more organic and articulate manner. The pyramids of Abusir had a core consisting of a step pyramid built with irregularly hewn stones, which in turn were dressed with blocks of squared limestone blocks. The mortuary temple to the east of the pyramid had a pre-established series of chambers: an entrance hall, a porticoed court with a basalt floor, a transverse corridor, a hall with five niches for the royal statues, an offerings hall with an altar and false door, an area with storerooms, and the cult pyramid in the south corner. Sculpted relief scenes and paintings decorated the walls of the temple, in which the pillars were replaced by columns whose capitals bore plant motifs. A typical example of this type of temple is the mortuary temple of Sahure', which has yielded some reliefs portraying the pharaoh victorious over his enemies or rows of gods bearing offerings.

The mortuary temple of Neuserre' on the other hand presented an innovation: a square chamber whose ceiling was supported by a single central column was placed between the hall with five niches and the offerings hall. Furthermore, on the northwest and southwest corners of the pyramid, two edifices in the shape of towers seem to herald the model of the entrance pylons in the temples constructed in a later epoch. Another very important innovation was introduced by Wenis, the last 5th-Dynasty pharaoh: the Pyramid Texts made their first appearance on the walls of the burial chamber of his pyramid at Saqqara.

The pyramids and mortuary temples built in the 6th Dynasty at Saqqara were modeled after the scheme established at Abusir by the preceding kings, with the sole exception of the pillars, which were again used in the mortuary temples in place of columns. It became common practice to place next to the pyramids the necropolises with the tombs of the royal family, especially the queens, who were buried in small pyramids with a mortuary temple.

60 LEFT AND BOTTOM RIGHT - THE INTERIOR WALLS OF THE PYRAMID OF UNAS AT SAQQARA ARE DECORATED WITH THE *PYRAMID TEXTS*, THE MOST ANCIENT COLLECTION OF RELIGIOUS FORMULAS IN EGYPTIAN LITERATURE.

60 BOTTOM LEFT - THE PYRAMID OF SAHURE' AT ABUSIR IS PRECEDED BY A MORTUARY TEMPLE THAT HAS TWO COLUMNS WITH PALM CAPITALS AND BY A PROCESSIONAL RAMP THAT WAS ONCE DECORATED WITH REFINED RELIEF SCULPTURE.

60-61 - VIEW FROM THE NORTHEAST OF THE NECROPOLIS OF ABUSIR IN WHICH ONE CAN RECOGNIZE, FROM THE RIGHT, THE PYRAMIDS OF SAHURE', NEUSERRE' AND NEFERIRKARE', THE UNFINISHED PYRAMID OF RA'NEFEREF, AND THE MASTABA OF PTAHSHEPSES.

THE BUILDERS OF THE PYRAMIDS

To this day it is difficult to explain how, armed only with archaic technology and human and animal labor, it was possible to build such colossal and technically precise monuments as the pyramids. Certain scenes, such as those decorating the processional avenue in the complex of Wenis at Saqqara, reveal how the transport of building material was effected – loaded onto boards by means of a system of ties and stays; on the ground, the blocks of stone were placed on wooden drags that were pulled with the aid of ropes or rolled on wooden beams. Much of the material used for the pyramids of Giza came from the local quarries that can still be seen. Only the outer casing of the pyramids, the limestone, was transported from the Tura quarries by boat, while the red granite used in the burial chambers and the lower casing of the pyramid of Menkaure' came from Aswan. Around the pyramids of Khufu and Khephren were found holes for poles that the architects probably used to check the correct positioning of the blocks of stone on the ground. The core of many pyramids is made up of rock, rubble and fill, on which the squared and finished stones of the casing were laid. Experts think that in order to lay the blocks of stone, the laborers used inclined ramps made of rubble and chalk. Numerous theories have been formulated regarding the shape of these ramps: they may have been single straight ramps that ascended toward the pyramid, or winding ramps that ran around the monument, built on each level as the construction work proceeded. Levers and stays were probably used only to position the smallest blocks on the vertex of the pyramid.

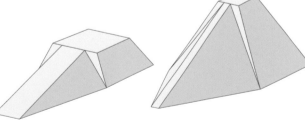

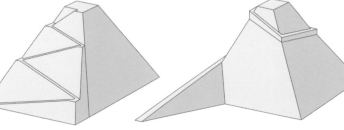

62-63 TOP - WORKMEN MAKING BRICKS IN THE TOMB OF REKHMIRE'.

62 AND 63 BOTTOM - THE DRAWINGS ILLUSTRATE THE POSSIBLE TYPES OF RAMP USED IN THE CONSTRUCTION OF THE PYRAMIDS.

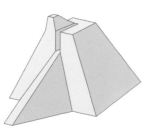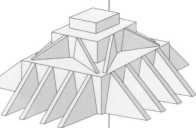

THE PRIVATE TOMBS AND STATUARY

The pyramids are the apogee of Egyptian architecture and the height of the symbolic expression of the concept of the Afterlife in the Old Kingdom, and they were built only for the pharaoh and the queens. Those citizens who belonged to the upper classes of ancient Egyptian society – nobles, princes or high-ranking officials connected with the court and the public administration – were allowed to build their tombs near those of the royal family. Thus, in the Old Kingdom, the royal funerary complexes were flanked by private necropolises, which were actual districts of tombs whose arrangement mirrored the composition of the social hierarchy. The necropolises still visible on the east and west sides of the Great Pyramid of Khufu, consisting of a grid layout of areas of tombs separated by perpendicular roads,

date from the 4th Dynasty. Officials, scribes and noblemen were buried in stone mastabas, which had a superstructure whose interior was arranged like that of a home, and an underground room used to house the sarcophagus of the deceased. A mortuary chapel guaranteed that the deceased would have a supply of offerings from the living that were placed in front of a false door, a sort of stele that looked like a wooden or stone door that served to link the world of the living and the world of the dead. The inner walls of the tomb and the offerings chapel were decorated with scenes of everyday life and with images of the deceased accompanied by his honorifics. One of the most ancient decorative motifs was the funerary banquet, with the deceased seated at an offerings table overflowing with food. This motif was first painted on steles and gradually began to be represented on the tomb walls, flanked by rows of offering bearers and scenes of food being prepared. The iconographic motifs of everyday life that abound on the walls of many Old Kingdom private tombs are arranged in horizontal registers and the individual scenes are often separated by large representations of the deceased. These themes belong to a canonical repertoire that includes scenes of farm work, animal husbandry, grape harvesting and wine-making, fishing,

bird and game hunting, and navigation. There are several scenes of animals being slaughtered: the haunches and hearts of cattle were an important part of the mortuary offerings because they were connected to the concept of rebirth. Since the deceased was a landowner, he was often portrayed inspecting the work of his artisans, who for the most part produced grave goods such as jewels, statues, sarcophagi, vases and wooden receptacles. Two of the decorative motifs most closely connected to the mortuary cult and beliefs were the "journey to the beautiful West," that is to say, the passage of the deceased to his tomb, and the hunt in the marsh together with his wife and children, which was another theme connected to the idea of rebirth.

Among the most ancient examples of wall painting in private tombs are those found in the mastabas connected to the funerary complex of Snofru at Maidum; the tomb of Neferma'at, the pharaoh's son, and his wife Itet, contained the celebrated representation of geese now kept in the Egyptian Museum, Cairo. During the reign of Khufu the decoration in private tombs was limited to a stele depicting the deceased's banquet, while the tomb decoration executed during the reign of the following 4th-Dynasty kings became more elaborate. However, the great development of architecture and private funerary painting took place in the 5th and 6th Dynasties. An example is the monumental tomb at Abusir of an official named Ptahshepses, who lived during the time of Neuserre'. The plan of his large mastaba was modeled after that of the royal mortuary temples and includes a porticoed entrance, a large courtyard with a columned cloister, an offerings hall, and a hall with niches for the statues of the deceased. The largest Old Kingdom mastabas are those of the 5th- and 6th-Dynasty dignitaries situated at Saqqara. The large rooms in their tombs are filled with splendid relief sculpture, whose colors, which in some cases are beautifully preserved, reveal the wide-ranging repertory of funerary motifs in the Old Kingdom.

64 - The deceased Werbau and Khentkawes are depicted seated at an offerings table in this relief that decorates the upper part of a false door-stele in the mastaba of Nefer at Saqqara (5th Dynasty).

65 top - The large mastaba of Ptahshepses at Abusir includes a set of chambers and spaces and among them a central courtyard with columns.

65 bottom - A reconstruction drawing showing a section of the west necropolis at Giza.

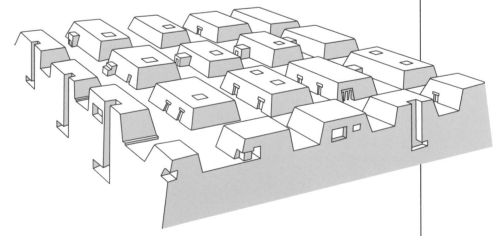

66 TOP LEFT AND BOTTOM – THE
MASTABA OF NEFERHERENPTAH AT
SAQQARA (5TH DYNASTY) IS KNOWN AS
THE 'TOMB OF THE BIRDS' BECAUSE OF
THE SCENES OF BIRD HUNTS AND THE
REPRESENTATION OF BIRDS TAKING
FLIGHT FROM A PAPYRUS STAND.

66 CENTER – A MULTICOLORED SCENE
ON A WALL OF THE MASTABA OF TIY AT
SAQQARA SHOWING MEN HUNTING
HIPPOPOTAMI IN THE MARSHES.

66-67 – MERERUKA, AN OFFICIAL
DURING THE REIGN OF TETI,
IS DEPICTED HERE WITH HIS MOTHER
AND WIFE WHILE HE OBSERVES ANIMALS
BEING FED AND BOATS BEING BUILT
IN THE LARGE HALL OF HIS MASTABA
AT SAQQARA.

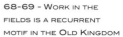
68-69 - WORK IN THE
FIELDS IS A RECURRENT
MOTIF IN THE OLD KINGDOM
TOMBS, AS IN THIS SCENE
FROM THE MASTABA
OF MEHU.

68 TOP LEFT - INSIDE THE
MASTABA OF MEHU AT
SAQQARA (EARLY 6TH
DYNASTY) ARE SCENES OF
FARM LIFE.

68 TOP RIGHT - THIS SCENE
FROM THE MASTABA OF MEHU
REPRESENTS THE MORTUARY
BARK THAT TRANSPORTS THE
MUMMY OF THE DECEASED.

69 TOP LEFT - THIS WOODEN MODEL (L. 23 1/2 IN, 60 CM), WHICH WAS FOUND IN THE TOMB OF NIANKHPEPI II AT MEIR (6TH DYNASTY), DEPICTS TWO WOMEN ENGAGED IN GRINDING GRAIN AND PREPARING THE FIRE (EGYPTIAN MUSEUM, CAIRO).

69 TOP RIGHT - A 6TH-DYNASTY WOODEN REPLICA (H. 9 1/2 IN, 24 CM) FROM MEIR OF A MAN COOKING A DUCK (EGYPTIAN MUSEUM, CAIRO).

The private Old Kingdom tombs have also yielded a great many statues that were usually placed inside the *serdab*, a niche cut out of the walls of the tomb. These statues portrayed the deceased, either alone or together with his wife and children, who were portrayed on a smaller scale. The figures were depicted standing, with one leg in front of the other as if walking, seated with their arms resting on their knees, or in the pose of a scribe, seated cross-legged with a papyrus roll on their knees. The Old Kingdom also produced statues of servants engaged in handicraft work. Among the most famous private statues executed in the Old Kingdom, mention should be made of the ones of the seated husband and wife Rahotep and Nofret, found in their mastaba at Maidum; the statue of the dwarf Seneb with his wife and children, from Giza; the wooden statue of the priest Ka'aper; the portrait of the architect of the pyramid of Khufu, Hemiunu; the famous scribe kept in the Louvre; and lastly, the statues of the priest Ranofer found at Saqqara, which are idealized representations of two phases of the deceased's life – youth and maturity.

70 - This sculpture (h. 17 in, 43 cm) portrays the dwarf Seneb and his family. Found in the deceased's mastaba at Giza, it dates to the period between the 5th and 6th Dynasty (Egyptian Museum, Cairo).

71 - This statue (h 18 1/4 in, 46.5 cm) portrays a personage buried at Giza during the 5th Dynasty in the typical pose of a scribe (University of Cairo Museum).

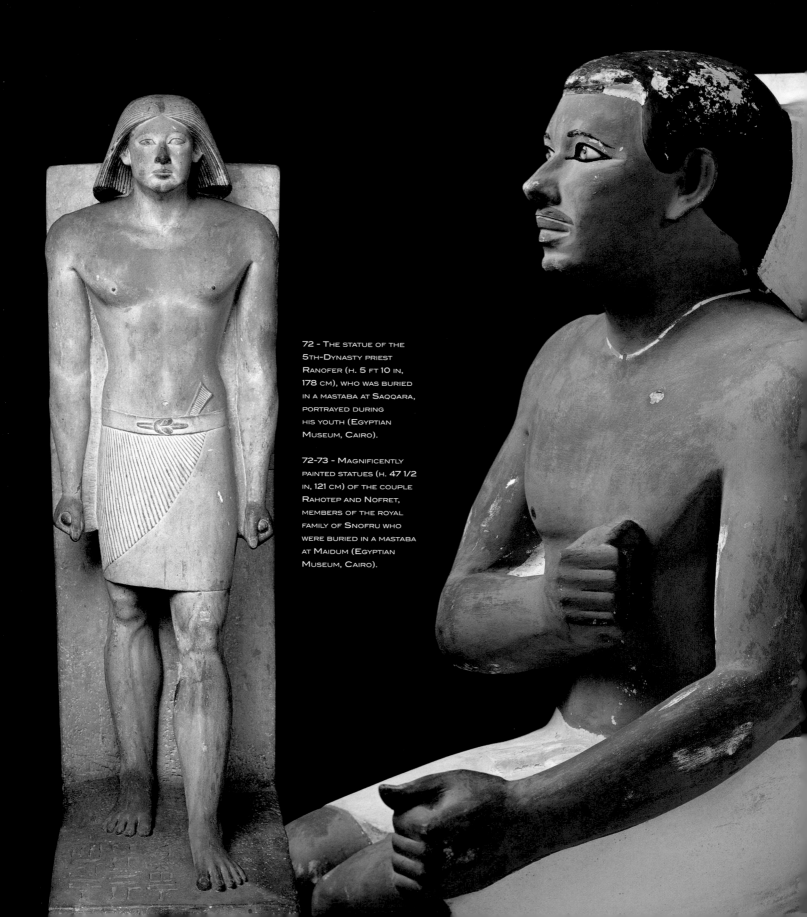

72 - THE STATUE OF THE
5TH-DYNASTY PRIEST
RANOFER (H. 5 FT 10 IN,
178 CM), WHO WAS BURIED
IN A MASTABA AT SAQQARA,
PORTRAYED DURING
HIS YOUTH (EGYPTIAN
MUSEUM, CAIRO).

72-73 - MAGNIFICENTLY
PAINTED STATUES (H. 47 1/2
IN, 121 CM) OF THE COUPLE
RAHOTEP AND NOFRET,
MEMBERS OF THE ROYAL
FAMILY OF SNOFRU WHO
WERE BURIED IN A MASTABA
AT MAIDUM (EGYPTIAN
MUSEUM, CAIRO).

THE CLASSICAL PERIOD: THE MIDDLE KINGDOM

THE FIRST INTERMEDIATE PERIOD AND THE MIDDLE KINGDOM

The collapse of central power at the end of the Old Kingdom triggered a long period of political fragmentation that scholars usually call the First Intermediate Period (2152–2065 BC). In this phase Memphis lost its role as the capital and political-economic fulcrum of the country, while there rose up various dynasties of local princes who controlled small regional territories and often struggled amongst themselves. Little is known about the 6th and 7th Dynasties, and even less is known about their kings except their names. In any case, we do know that their power must have been limited to the Memphite area, since the Delta was then occupied by tribes of Asian Bedouins and Middle Egypt was controlled by the local dynasty of Herakleopolis, which founded the 9th and 10th Dynasties. Very soon these dynasties clashed with the Theban princes who founded the 11th Dynasty. The victor in the struggle for supremacy in the middle Nile Valley was Inyotef II of Thebes, who extended dominion from the First Cataract to the Asyut region. But it was this pharaoh's successor, Mentuhotpe II, who succeeded in unifying Egypt once again, giving rise to the Middle Kingdom.

Artistic production in the First Intermediate Period has provincial features that betray the lack of centralized workshops. Our main source of information in this period are the tombs of the provincial governors (nomarchs) at Asyut, Beni Hasan, Meir, Deir el-Bersha and Qaw el-Kebir. Typical products of the First Intermediate Period are the wooden models depicting scenes of everyday life, which were part of the deceased's grave goods. In the tomb of Mesehti at Asyut archaeologists found the famous models of two battalions of the Egyptian army, consisting of Egyptian lancers and Nubian archers.

The Theban prince Mentuhotpe II (2065–2014 BC) defeated the dynasts of Herakleopolis and reunified Egypt, giving rise to a long period of peace and prosperity in the country, during which the most important texts in Egyptian literature were written and the foundations were laid for artistic models that were imitated for a very long time. Mentuhotpe II chose his birthplace Thebes as the capital of his kingdom, which during his reign went through a first phase of monumental construction. This pharaoh is remembered most of all for the funerary complex he built on the west bank of Thebes, at the foot of the rocky cliff of Deir el-Bahri. Here he built a temple in the valley, from which departed a long ascending ramp that went toward the rock face and the mortuary temple. The ramp gave access to a tree-lined forecourt where the archaeologist Howard Carter discovered the entrance to an underground cenotaph (Bab el-Hosan), in which he found an empty sarcophagus and a statue of the king, depicted with a dark complexion and wearing *Sed* festival attire. At the end of the court another ramp gave access to a large terrace preceded by a double colonnade with pillars. An exterior ambulatory supported by columns encircled a peristyle with pillars that ran on all four sides of the terrace. In the middle of this space was a structure connected to the solar cult, which may have looked like a tumulus or small pyramid. At the end of the terrace were the rock-hewn funerary shafts of six queens of the reign of Mentuhotpe II with their respective shrines. The tombs of the queens Ashayt and Kauit had two decorated sarcophagi that are now in the Egyptian Museum, Cairo. Behind the terrace was the mortuary temple proper, consisting of a hypostyle hall with 82 pillars, access to which was gained by means of a peristyle court. A corridor under the hypostyle led to the tomb of Mentuhotpe II, which was cut out of the cliff rock.

After the brief rules of Mentuhotpe III and IV, the throne passed on to the 12th Dynasty (1994–1781 BC), founded by Amenemhet I (1994–1964 BC). The new dynasts shifted the capital from Thebes to a more northerly city near el-Lisht, the newly founded Itjtawy, in the Faiyum area. After Amenemhet I was assassinated in a court conspiracy, he was succeeded by his son Senwosret I (1964–1929 BC), who had already been coregent with his father. Senwosret I continued the military campaigns begun by his father against the Libyans and Nubians, and in the southern region began the construction of a series of fortresses to defend the Egyptian border and the country's trade traffic. An obelisk of Senwosret I at Heliopolis is all that remains of the building program carried out by this ruler in the religious center of the cult of the sun god Re'. At Thebes, on the other hand, the pharaoh built at Karnak a small limestone temple known as the White Chapel, which lies on a platform and is accessible by means of two ramps. The chapel was supported by 16 pillars and had carved reliefs with scenes and cult inscriptions dedicated to the Theban god Amun. During the reign of Amenemhet II (1929–1898 BC) there were diplomatic and commercial relations with the Near East and the Minoan civilization, which are attested by the Egyptian jewels found at Byblos, a treasure trove of Syrian silver objects found in the Temple of Montu at Tod, and Kamares pottery found in Egypt. Senwosret II (1898–1881 BC) devoted his efforts to public works, the main one being the reclamation of the vast Faiyum oasis, connected to the Nile by a canal dug precisely during the Middle Kingdom. To the east of the pyramid that this pharaoh had built at Lahun, archaeologists brought to light the village of the laborers and artisans who worked on the construction of the royal necropolis, the only known example of a Middle Kingdom residential area. The village of Kahun (or el-Lahun), which has a rectangular layout and is encircled by walls, was divided into three main districts. The one facing west had large houses with many rooms around a central courtyard and was reserved for the foremen and the most important workmen. The east quarter was occupied by small, closely packed houses and used by the simple laborers. An elevated area housed the village temple and perhaps a royal palace. Kahun has provided us with important papyri containing information on the activity of the workmen's community and on the administration of the mortuary temple, as well as on medical, veterinarian and juridical practice.

78 - THIS OSIRIAN PILLAR OF SENWOSRET I (H. 7 FT 10 IN, 239 CM) ONCE DECORATED THE PROCESSIONAL RAMP OF THE FUNERARY COMPLEX OF EL-LISHT (EGYPTIAN MUSEUM, CAIRO).

79 - WOODEN HEAD OF A WOMAN (H. 4 IN, 10.5 CM) WEARING A WIG WITH GILDED INLAY DISCOVERED IN THE FUNERARY COMPLEX OF AMENEMHET I AT EL-LISHT (EGYPTIAN MUSEUM, CAIRO).

The reign of Senwosret III (1881–1842 BC) marked the high point of the Middle Kingdom. The Egyptian army penetrated into Nubia, arriving as far as the Second Cataract zone, where the pharaoh built a series of forts to defend the border and control the course of the Nile against the threat of the Kerma kingdom in Nubia, which lay in the Third Cataract area. The sculptural portraits of Senwosret III reveal a sovereign with an elderly and austere face, with high cheekbones and hollowed cheeks. The meaning of this stylistic choice by the artists was based on the desire to underscore the pharaoh's firm commitment and sense of responsibility as leader of his nation and people. The last great pharaoh in the Middle Kingdom was Amenemhet III (1842–1794 BC), who completed the reclamation of the Faiyum Oasis and carried out a building program there. At Biahmu the pharaoh had two colossal statues sculpted, whose pedestals have been preserved, while at Medinet Madi he built a temple dedicated to the goddess of harvest and childbirth Renenutet and the crocodile god Sobek. There are some statues of Amenemhet III whose archaic style and austere features are typical of the final phase of the Middle Kingdom; among these are the sphinxes found at Tanis and a magnificent copper bust discovered in the funerary complex of Hawara. The 12th Dynasty ended with the brief reigns of Amenemhet IV and Queen Nefrusobk, just before Egypt once again plunged into political chaos, which this time was brought about by the power takeover by an Asiatic people, the Hyksos.

THE ROYAL NECROPOLISES

After the innovative funerary complex that Mentuhotpe II had built at Thebes, the 12th-Dynasty kings returned to the traditional Memphite pyramid adopted in the Old Kingdom. The Middle Kingdom pyramids, unlike the earlier ones, were not built of solid stone, but were made by filling a stone supporting structure with bricks and rubble, which is the reason why they are now in such a poor state of preservation. The pyramid was topped by a *pyramidion*, or capstone, a block of diorite or basalt decorated with inscriptions, like the capstone from the pyramid of Amenemhet III at Dahshur, now in the Egyptian Museum, Cairo. Amenemhet I and Senwosret I were buried at el-Lisht, where officials and members of the royal family were also interred. The plan of the mortuary temples of these two kings is similar to those built in the 5th and 6th Dynasties.

A few ruins are all that remains of the pyramid of Amenemhet II at Dahshur, but this pharaoh's funerary complex has yielded the precious treasure belonging to two princesses, Khnemt and Iti, who were buried in two shaft tombs on the west side of the pyramid. Among the gold and semiprecious

stone jewelry found in their tombs there are two diadems belonging to Princess Khnumet, a choker decorated with a double falcon's head, bracelets, pendants, necklaces, clasps, anklets and an elegant dagger with a decorated handle belonging to Princess Iti. The pyramid of Senwosret II at el-Lahun seems to be unfinished, but south of the pyramid, the shaft tomb of Princess Sit-Hathor-Iunet contained some finely wrought jewelry originally kept in ebony boxes, including a Hathoric mirror and the queen's diadem crown, as well as an inlaid pectoral with the cartouche of Amenemhet II.

Senwosret III had two tombs built for himself: a pyramid at Dahshur and an underground tomb at Abydos with its respective mortuary temple. The funerary complex of Dahshur, built near Snofru's Red Pyramid, includes a small mortuary temple on the east side of the pyramid and a larger sanctuary south of the complex. In the funerary precinct there are also seven small pyramids that were the tombs of seven queens, in whose underground chambers archaeologists found the jewels that belonged to the princesses Sithathor and Merit, which included necklaces, bracelets, anklets, pendants, belts and pectorals with inscriptions. In 1994, in the shaft tomb of the queen mother Weret II, which was hewn out of the rock under southwest corner of the pyramid, archaeologist brought to light yet another trove of jewels as well as the queen's sarcophagus.

Amenemhet III built his first pyramid (known as the Black Pyramid) at Dahshur, whose brick nucleus has only survived. The underground chambers have a rather complicated layout consisting of two levels of rooms used as the tombs of the pharaoh and two queens. Other royal family tombs are situated along the north side of the pyramid, where the tomb of a 13th-Dynasty pharaoh, Awibre' Hor, was also hewn out of the earth; this latter had a wooden statue placed in a *naos* that has been preserved. However, some structural faults in the underground chambers forced Amenemhet III to abandon this complex and begin the construction of another tomb at the site of Hawara, in the Faiyum. Today, these underground chambers are flooded with groundwater and almost nothing remains of the large temple complex south of the pyramid, which in antiquity was known as a "labyrinth."

82-83 - THE CENTRAL CORE OF THE PYRAMID OF SENWOSRET II AT EL-LAHUN HAS BEEN PRESERVED, WHILE THE OUTERMOST WALLS COLLAPSED. EIGHT MASTABAS FOR THE ROYAL FAMILY AND A SMALL SUBSIDIARY PYRAMID WERE CONSTRUCTED ALONG THE NORTH SIDE OF THIS MONUMENT.

83 TOP - AN AERIAL VIEW OF THE SITE OF DAHSHUR SHOWING THE PYRAMID-CENOTAPH OF AMENEMHET III, WHOSE BRICK NUCLEUS HAS ONLY SURVIVED, AND, IN THE BACKGROUND, THE BENT PYRAMID OF SNOFRU.

83 BOTTOM - THE PYRAMID OF AMENEMHET I AT EL-LISHT WAS BUILT BY PUTTING BRICKS AND RUBBLE IN THE SPACE BETWEEN THE STONE WALLS SET DIAGONALLY AGAINST THE CORE OF THE MONUMENT.

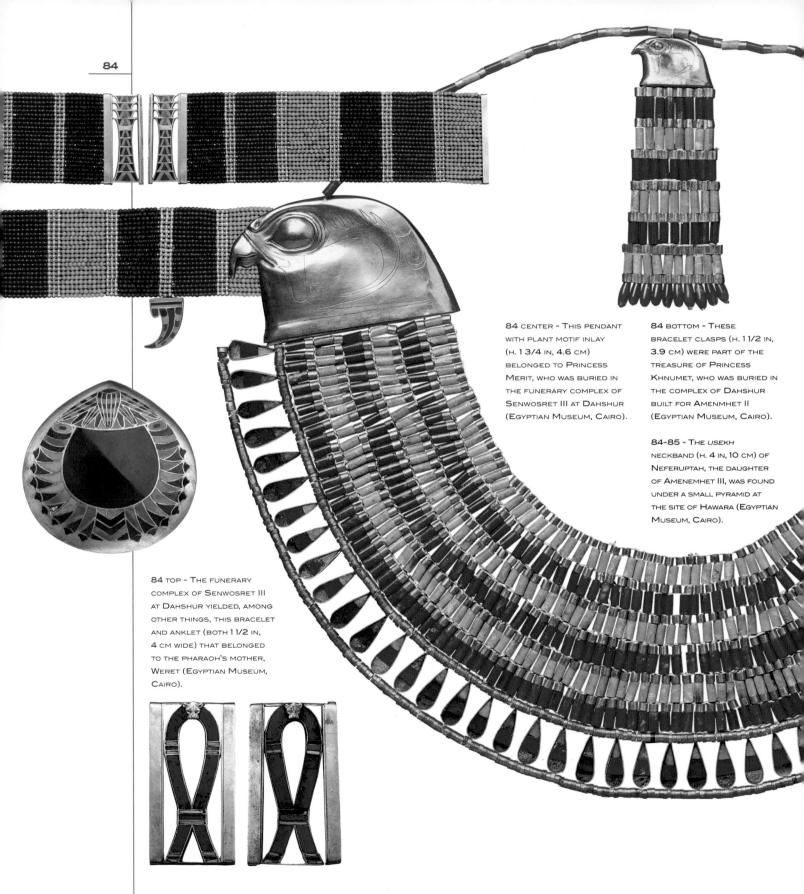

84 CENTER - THIS PENDANT WITH PLANT MOTIF INLAY (H. 1 3/4 IN, 4.6 CM) BELONGED TO PRINCESS MERIT, WHO WAS BURIED IN THE FUNERARY COMPLEX OF SENWOSRET III AT DAHSHUR (EGYPTIAN MUSEUM, CAIRO).

84 BOTTOM - THESE BRACELET CLASPS (H. 1 1/2 IN, 3.9 CM) WERE PART OF THE TREASURE OF PRINCESS KHNUMET, WHO WAS BURIED IN THE COMPLEX OF DAHSHUR BUILT FOR AMENMHET II (EGYPTIAN MUSEUM, CAIRO).

84-85 - THE *USEKH* NECKBAND (H. 4 IN, 10 CM) OF NEFERUPTAH, THE DAUGHTER OF AMENEMHET III, WAS FOUND UNDER A SMALL PYRAMID AT THE SITE OF HAWARA (EGYPTIAN MUSEUM, CAIRO).

84 TOP - THE FUNERARY COMPLEX OF SENWOSRET III AT DAHSHUR YIELDED, AMONG OTHER THINGS, THIS BRACELET AND ANKLET (BOTH 1 1/2 IN, 4 CM WIDE) THAT BELONGED TO THE PHARAOH'S MOTHER, WERET (EGYPTIAN MUSEUM, CAIRO).

85 TOP - THESE BRACELETS (H. 1 1/4-3/4 IN, 3.3-1.9 CM) ALSO BELONGED TO THE CACHE OF QUEEN KHNUMET. THEIR CLASPS ARE IN THE SHAPE OF AUSPICIOUS HIEROGLYPHS (EGYPTIAN MUSEUM, CAIRO).

85 BOTTOM LEFT - THIS PECTORAL PORTRAYS TWO FALCON-HEADED SPHINXES DEFEATING THEIR ENEMIES AND A VULTURE PROTECTING THE CARTOUCHE OF SENWOSRET III (EGYPTIAN MUSEUM, CAIRO).

85 BOTTOM RIGHT - A URAEUS (H. 2 1/2 IN, 6.7 CM) FOUND IN THE PYRAMID OF SENWOSRET II AT EL-LAHUN (EGYPTIAN MUSEUM, CAIRO).

THE PRIVATE NECROPOLISES

During the Old Kingdom, the dignitaries and court officials were usually buried in the royal necropolises, next to the pyramids of the pharaohs whom they had served. With the anarchy and political fragmentation that occurred after the 6th Dynasty, many provincial governors (nomes) began to have themselves buried in their regions of origin, a custom that continued throughout the Middle Kingdom as well. In the rocky hills that bound the west bank of the Thebes region, rock-hewn tombs (*saff*) preceded by large courts were constructed. Their façades had a series of apertures cut out of the rock that gave access to a transverse corridor and a hall with pillars, under which the burial chamber proper was excavated. One of the private Middle Kingdom tombs at Deir el-Bahri, which belonged to the functionary Meketre', who lived in the early 12th Dynasty, yielded precisely wrought wooden models of everyday scenes: carrying

out a census of the livestock, navigation and fishing along the river, artisans at work in their workshops. These models, which were made to accompany the deceased in the Afterlife, represent the transposition in three dimensions of the scenes painted on the walls of the tombs dating from as long before as the Old Kingdom. Other rock-cut tombs were built by the local governors of Elephantine (Aswan) in the necropolis of Qubbet el-Hawa, which had been used in the 6th Dynasty. One of the largest and most finely decorated tombs in the necropolis is the one belonging to Sarenput II, the military commander at Elephantine during the reign of Amenemhet II.

The region of Middle Egypt has provided us with the best examples of provincial tombs built in the Middle Kingdom. At Beni Hasan a series of rock-cut tombs were made for the local overlords of the XVI Egyptian nome on the slopes of the

eastern hills. Preceded by outer courts with a two-pillar portico, these tombs consisted of several halls supported by lotus stem columns or pillars. The tombs of the overlords Baqet III, Khety, Amenemhet and Khnumhotpe II contain many paintings with scenes of everyday life (hunting, fishing, bird hunting, handicrafts activity, dance, a collection of papyrus rolls, animal husbandry) or funerary scenes; strikingly original examples of this art are the representations of wrestlers exercising. The tomb of Khnumhotep II, who lived during the reign of Senwosret II, contains a famous scene of a group of Asiatic dignitaries on a trade mission in Egypt. Other rock-cut provincial tombs lie in the necropolises of Deir el-Bersha, Meir, Asyut and Qaw el-Kebir, where the governors of the tenth nome of Egypt built monumental tombs whose layout reminds one of the funerary complexes of the pharaohs' pyramids.

86-87 - A WOODEN MODEL (H. 21 1/2 IN, 55 CM) DISCOVERED IN THE TOMB OF MEKETRE' AT DEIR EL-BAHRI (11TH–12TH DYNASTY), DEPICTING A SCENE OF EVERYDAY LIFE: THE DECEASED IS UNDER A PAVILION AND IS SUPERVISING THE COUNT OF HIS LIVESTOCK (EGYPTIAN MUSEUM, CAIRO).

87 TOP - IN THE TOMB AT BENI HASAN OF KHNUMHOTPE II, THE PROVINCIAL GOVERNOR DURING THE REIGNS OF AMENEMHET II AND SENWOSRET III, IS THIS PAINTED SCENE SHOWING SOME ASIATIC DIGNITARIES LEADING THEIR LIVESTOCK DURING A TRADE MISSION.

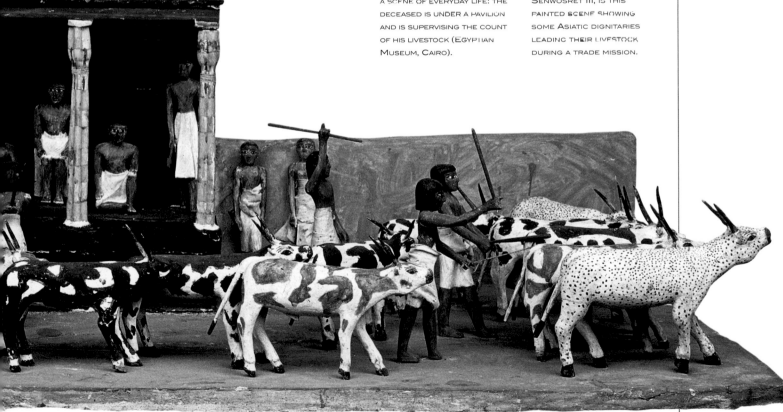

88 TOP LEFT - THIS WOODEN
REPLICA (H. 17 IN, 43 CM) OF A
HOUSE WITH A PORTICO AND GARDEN
COMES FROM THE TOMB OF THE
OFFICIAL MEKETRE' AT DEIR EL-
BAHRI (EGYPTIAN MUSEUM, CAIRO).

88 TOP RIGHT AND 89 -
MEKETRE'S TOMB YIELDED THESE
REPLICAS (H. 9 3/4 – 10 IN,

25–26 CM) OF EGYPTIAN WEAVING
AND CARPENTRY WORKSHOPS
(EGYPTIAN MUSEUM, CAIRO).

88 BOTTOM - A MODEL (L. 30 1/2
IN, 78 CM) FOUND IN THE COMPLEX
OF MENTUHOTPE II AT DEIR EL-
BAHRI, SHOWS THE VARIOUS
PHASES OF BREAD-MAKING
(BRITISH MUSEUM, LONDON).

90-91 - Two boats being
used for fishing are the
subject of yet another
replica (h. 1 ft, 31.5 cm)
discovered in the tomb of
Meketre' (Egyptian
Museum, Cairo).

91 top - This replica of a
sailboat (h. 4 ft, 124 cm),
which came from the tomb
of Meketre', is maneuvered
by a crew commanded by a
person wielding a cane
(Egyptian Museum, Cairo).

91 center - Model of a
bark (h. 2 ft, 61 cm)
transporting Meketre',
who is seated under a
baldachin (Egyptian
Museum, Cairo).

THE EMPIRE OF THE PHARAOHS:
THE NEW KINGDOM

The end of the 12th Dynasty was marked by a new period of political anarchy in Egypt that scholars call the Second Intermediate Period (1781–1550 BC). In the Delta, the Semitic peoples of Asiatic origin that ancient Egyptian documents indicate as *heqau-khasut* ("rulers of foreign lands," and "Hyksos" in Greek) took advantage of the political weakness of the 13th and 14th Dynasties and seized the reins of power. The Hyksos rulers made Avaris (Tell el-Dab'a), in the eastern Delta, their capital, from which they ruled the northern part of Egypt and even had themselves recognized as legitimate pharaohs (15th and 16th Dynasties) and honored the Egyptian gods, especially Seth. Together with the Hyksos, new technology and new techniques in metalworking also arrived in Egypt, which facilitated the spread of more resistant and efficient weapons as well as the introduction of the war chariot and the composite bow. Animal husbandry, ceramics production and textile manufacture also benefited from improved techniques imported from abroad. Opposition to the Hyksos government began to be organized by the princes of Thebes of the 16th Dynasty (1650–1550 BC), who had control over Upper Egypt. The decisive struggles for supremacy of the country took place during the reign of the Thebans Seqenenre'-Ta'o II, Kamose and 'Ahmose (1550–1525 BC). It was 'Ahmose who drove the Hyksos out of the Delta for good and put an end to the Second Intermediate Period, thus inaugurating the 18th Dynasty and with it a new phase in ancient Egyptian history – the New Kingdom. Traces of the tombs of the 17th-Dynasty kings have been preserved in the Theban necropolis of Dra Abu el-Naga', a site that yielded the rich grave goods found in the tomb of Queen Ahhotep, the mother of Kamose and 'Ahmose. Among the objects in this treasure are the queen's sarcophagus and jewels, some ceremonial weapons that belonged to 'Ahmose, and precious metal models of boats. Another woman played a special role in the transition to the New Kingdom: Queen 'Ahmose-Nefertiry, 'Ahmose's wife and the first queen to bear the title of Divine Consort, whose wooden mummy-shaped sarcophagus has been preserved.

93 - THIS STATUE OF RAMESSES II (H. 6 FT 4 IN, 194 CM) IS A MASTERPIECE OF EGYPTIAN ART (EGYTPIAN MUSEUM, TURIN).

94 - THE LID OF THE GILDED WOOD SARCOPHAGUS OF QUEEN AHHOTEP (L. 7 FT, 212 CM) WAS FOUND IN A TOMB AT DRA ABU EL-NAGA' (EGYPTIAN MUSEUM, CAIRO).

95 - 'AHMOSE-NEFERTIRY WAS BURIED IN A SARCOPHAGUS (L. 12 1/2 FT, 378 CM) IN THE DEIR EL-BAHRI CACHE (EGYPTIAN MUSEUM, CAIRO).

THE TUTHMOSID KINGS

Amenhotep I (1525–1504 BC), the second pharaoh in the 18th Dynasty, continued the pacification policy begun by his father and led some expeditions into Nubia. He restored and built several Egyptian temples, especially at Karnak, where some of his relief sculptures still exist. We do not know for certain whether this pharaoh was buried in a tomb in the Dra Abu el-Naga' necropolis or inaugurated the royal necropolis in the Valley of the Kings (*Biban el-Muluk*). A small mortuary temple dedicated to Amenhotep I and his mother, 'Ahmose-Nefertiry, was built in the plain opposite the necropolis of Dra Abu el-Naga', thus initiating the series of the "temples of millions of years" that the New Kingdom pharaohs built on the west bank of Thebes in the following centuries. His successor Tuthmosis I (1504–1492 BC) is remembered for having led military campaigns in Syria and Nubia and for having partly built the Temple of Amun at Karnak.

Tuthmosis I was the first pharaoh who was certainly buried in the Valley of the Kings. He was first interred in Tomb KV 20, where he also had his daughter Hatshepsut buried. His mummy was later transferred to Tomb KV 38 by his grandson Tuthmosis III. Tuthmosis II (1492–1479 BC), the son of a secondary consort of Tuthmosis I, married his ambitious half-sister Hatshepsut in order to legitimize his ascent to the throne. Traces of his short-lived reign are to be found at Karnak and in the Nubian temples of Semna and Buhen. When he died, his son Tuthmosis III was too young to ascend to the throne and Queen Hatshepsut (1479–1458 BC) acted as regent, later proclaiming herself the sole ruler of Egypt and having herself portrayed as a pharaoh in male attire. Besides leaving her name at Karnak, Hatshepsut had a small temple, the Speos Artemidos, cut out of the rock in the Beni Hasan area and dedicated it to the lioness goddess Pakhet.

96 - This painted limestone head from Karnak (h. 1 ft 10 in, 58 cm) is probably a portrait of Amenhotep I wearing the white crown of Upper Egypt (Luxor Museum).

97 - A painted limestone head (h. 2 ft, 61 cm) of Queen Hatshepsut with facial features of a man was part of a statue erected in the mortuary temple of Deir el-Bahri (Egyptian Museum, Cairo).

The most famous work commissioned by this queen is the mortuary temple built at the foot of the rocky amphitheater of Deir el-Bahri, next to the one of Mentuhotpe II. The work of the architect Senenmut, the queen's favorite tutor for her daughter Neferu-re', the temple has a series of three terraces on different levels that are framed by porticoes (or colonnades) supported

by pillars and connected by a ramp that leads to a valley temple. The porticoes are decorated with painted relief sculpture: the first shows the construction of obelisks at Karnak as well as ritual hunting and fishing scenes; the second presents a commercial expedition to the land of Punt and the divine birth of the queen as the daughter of the god Amun; the third is decorated with Osiride pillars and colossal statues of the queen. The middle terrace gives access to two shrines dedicated to the goddess Hathor and the god Anubis. The third portico affordes access to the heart of the sanctuary, where a large hypostyle hall is decorated with religious scenes, and to two shrines dedicated to Re'-Harakhty and to the funerary cult of Hatshepsut and Tuthmosis I. The wall at the end of the hall leads to a small rock-hewn sanctuary dedicated to the god Amon, on whose wall Hatshepsut and Tuthmosis III are portrayed while making offerings to the god.

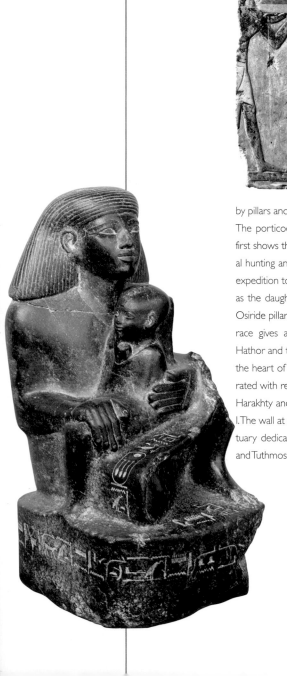

98 LEFT - SENENMUT (H. 23 1/2 IN, 60 CM) HOLDS UP NEFERU-RE', HATSHEPSUT'S DAUGHTER (EGYPTIAN MUSEUM, CAIRO).

98 RIGHT - THE DEIR EL-BAHRI RELIEF (H. 19 1/4 IN, 49 CM) SHOWS THE KING AND QUEEN OF PUNT (EGYPTIAN MUSEUM, CAIRO).

98-99 - THE ROCK FACE OF DEIR EL-BAHRI IS THE SETTING FOR THE TEMPLES OF HATSHEPSUT AND MENTUHOTPE II.

100-101 - THE UPPER PORTICO OF THE MORTUARY TEMPLE OF HATSHEPSUT AT DEIR EL-BAHRI WAS DECORATED WITH OSIRIAN STATUES OF THE QUEEN (WEARING THE DOUBLE CROWN OF EGYPT) THAT RESTED ON THE 24 PILLARS.

Although the true identity of a mummy believed by some to be Hatshepsut is still being debated, it is known that upon her death the throne passed to Tuthmosis III (1479–1425 BC), whose military campaigns turned Egypt into an international empire in the Near East. The *Annals* of the 17 military campaigns led by Tuthmosis III were carved on the walls of a hall near the bark sanctuary of the Temple of Karnak. The Egyptian army fought on several occasions along the Palestinian coast and in Syria against the powerful Mitanni Empire, a Hurrian state that dominated the upper course of the Tigris and the Euphrates. Besides being a major military triumph for the pharaoh, the conquest of the city of Megiddo after months of siege provided him with precious booty; this exploit was illustrated on Pylon VI at Karnak. Tuthmosis III also headed military campaigns in Nubia (Kush) where, by defeating the Kerma kingdom, he extended Egyptian hegemony as far as the Fourth Cataract area. In Nubia he built the temples of 'Amada, Buhen and Semna and ordered the excavation of the rock-cut chapel of el-Lessiya, which is now kept in the Egyptian Museum, Turin. He also founded the city of Napata at the foot of Gebel Barkal. At Deir el-Bahri Tuthmosis III dedicated a small sanctuary to Amun, which he erected between the mortuary temples of Mentuhotpe II and Hatshepsut; a shrine in this complex, which has preserved its fine polychrome decoration and was dedicated to the goddess Hathor, is now in the Egyptian Museum, Cairo. Tuthmosis III is buried in the Valley of the Kings (Tomb KV 34), but also built a mortuary temple for himself south of Deir el-Bahri that is now in a state of total ruin.

102 - THIS SMALL POLYCHROME CHAPEL (H. 7 FT 4 IN, 225 CM), WHOSE VAULT IS DECORATED WITH A STAR-STUDDED SKY, WAS DEDICATED TO AMUN-RE' AND HATHOR AND WAS PART OF THE TEMPLE BUILT BY TUTHMOSIS III AT DEIR EL-BAHRI (EGYPTIAN MUSEUM, CAIRO).

103 - THIS SPLENDID GREY GRANITE STATUE (H. 3 FT, 90.5 CM) FOUND IN THE KARNAK CACHE DEPICTS TUTHMOSIS III AS A YOUNG MAN (LUXOR MUSEUM).

104-105 - The burial chamber in the tomb of Tuthmosis III is oval shaped and is supported by two pillars with decorations taken from the *Litany of Re'*.

105 top - Tuthmosis III is suckled by the goddess Hathor in the guise of a sycamore tree in this scene painted on a pillar in his burial chamber.

105 center - The walls of the burial chamber of Tuthmosis III are painted with texts and illustrations from the *Book of the Dead* and are presented like an open papyrus scroll.

105 bottom - The *Book of the Dead*, illustrated here in the tomb of Tuthmosis III, is accompanied by scenes describing the journey of the sun god through the hours of the night in the Afterlife.

Amenhotep II (1424–1397 BC) pursued his father's military campaigns against the Mitanni kingdom, which ended with the drawing up of a peace treaty, and carried on the building program in Nubia that Tuthmosis III had begun. At Giza he erected a small temple northeast of the Great Sphinx that was associated with the sun god Horemakhet. This ruler was particularly famous for his athletic prowess, so much so that in some representations he was depicted riding his chariot with the reins tied around his waist and shooting arroes expertly into a bronze target. In 1898, archaeologists found several New Kingdom royal mummies in his tomb in the Valley of the Kings (KV 35) that had been hidden by 21th-Dynasty priests so they would not be violated by the frequent pillaging of the Theban necropolis. Tuthmosis IV (1397–1387 BC) is famous for the stele (the so-called dream stele) that he had placed at the foot of the Great Sphinx of Giza after having completed restoration work on the monument. He also built the largest known Egyptian obelisk, which now stands in Piazza San Giovanni Laterano, in Rome. His tomb in the Valley of the Kings (KV 43) is decorated with rows of divinities.

106 - AMENHOTEP II (H. 4 FT 1 IN, 125 CM) IS PROTECTED BY THE COBRA GODDESS MERESGER ("THE LOVER OF SILENCE"), WHO HAS THE SUN DISK BETWEEN HATHORIC HORNS. THIS GODDESS WAS CONNECTED TO THE THEBAN NECROPOLIS (EGYPTIAN MUSEUM, CAIRO).

107 – A STATUE (H. 3 FT 9 IN, 115 CM) FROM KARNAK PORTRAYING TUTHMOSIS IV SEATED ON HIS THRONE TOGETHER WITH THE QUEEN MOTHER TEO. THE PHARAOH IS TREADING ON NINE BOWS, THE SYMBOLS OF THE ENEMIES OF EGYPT (EGYPTIAN MUSEUM, CAIRO).

The reign of Amenhotep III (1387–1350 BC) marked the apogee of artistic expression in the 18th Dynasty and was a period of peace and prosperity for Egypt. He married a woman named Teye, the daughter of a noble family from Akhmim: a colossal statue of the king together with his wife and three daughters is now on display at the Egyptian Museum, Cairo. Teye's parents, Yuia and Tuia, were buried in a modest tomb in the Valley of the Kings (KV 46) where luxurious grave goods were discovered. Amenhotep III was a great builder, thanks to the tireless activity of the court architect Amenhotep, Son of Hapu, who was granted the honor of being allowed to construct his mortuary temple next to those of the pharaohs. At Thebes, in the locality of el-Malqata, the pharaoh had a huge royal palace complex built that included temples and residences for the royal family and that still has some naturalistic floor decoration. Amenhotep III also did some building work in the Temple of Amun at Karnak and founded the Temple of Luxor, in whose court a colossal statue of the pharaoh on a sort of drag was discovered in 1989. In Nubia he built a rock-cut temple at el-Sebu'a, another temple at Kawa, and two sanctuaries dedicated to the deified figures of himself and of his consort Teye at Soleb and Sedeinga. The mortuary temple the pharaoh had built on the west bank of Thebes was truly enormous, but unfortunately all that remains of this monument are the foundations and the two colossal statues that once stood on either side of the entrance pylon – the so-called Memnon Colossi. The pharaoh was buried in Tomb KV 22 of the Valley of the Kings after a long and peaceful reign.

108 LEFT - A CLAY HEAD (H. 15 IN, 38 CM) OF AMENHOTEP III WEARING THE BLUE CROWN (EGYPTIAN MUSEUM, CAIRO).

108 RIGHT - TEYE WAS ONE OF THE MOST POWERFUL QUEENS IN ANCIENT EGYPT DESPITE THE FACT THAT SHE WAS NOT OF ROYAL

BLOOD (EGYPTIAN MUSEUM, CAIRO).

109 -AN ALABASTRINE CALCITE STATUE (H. 8 FT 2 IN, 250 CM) OF THE CROCODILE GOD SOBEK, WEARING THE ATEF CROWN AND PROTECTING AMENHOTEP III (LUXOR MUSEUM).

110 TOP - THE SO-CALLED MEMNON COLOSSI WERE REALLY STATUES, ABOUT 65 1/2 FT (20 M) HIGH, DEPICTING THE ENTHRONED AMENHOTEP III AND PLACED AT THE ENTRANCE OF HIS MORTUARY TEMPLE.

110 BOTTOM - THIS SCULPTURE GROUP (H. 23 FT, 7 M), WHICH ORIGINALLY STOOD IN THE MORTUARY TEMPLE OF AMENHOTEP III, REPRESENTS THE KING ON HIS THRONE, ACCOMPANIED BY QUEEN TEYE AND THREE OF THEIR DAUGHTERS (EGYPTIAN MUSEUM, CAIRO).

110-111 - AMENHOTEP III'S TEMPLE OF MILLIONS OF YEARS STOOD IN THE PLAIN IN WEST THEBES, IT WAS VERY LARGE AND WAS DECORATED WITH SEVERAL STATUES.

112 LEFT - THIS GILDED WOOD SARCOPHAGUS (L. 6 1/2 FT, 204 CM) CONTAINED THE MUMMY OF YUIA, THE FATHER OF QUEEN TEYE. HIS CHEST IS COVERED WITH A FINE INLAY OF PRECIOUS STONES AND VITREOUS PASTE DEPICTING A NECKBAND AND A VULTURE WITH OUTSPREAD WINGS (EGYPTIAN MUSEUM, CAIRO).

112 RIGHT - THE DEATH MASK OF TUIA (H. 15 IN, 40 CM) WAS FOUND, TOGETHER WITH ABUNDANT GRAVE GOODS, IN THE TOMB IN THE VALLEY OF THE KINGS (KV 46) HEWN OUT OF THE ROCK FOR THE ROYAL COUPLE (EGYPTIAN MUSEUM, CAIRO).

112-113 - THESE FOUR LIMESTONE VASES (H. 10 IN, 25 CM) FROM THE GRAVE REGALIA OF YUIA HAVE UNUSUAL LIDS IN THE SHAPE OF ANIMALS (EGYPTIAN MUSEUM, CAIRO).

113 TOP - THIS GOLD LEAF MIRROR SPECULAR PORTRAIT OF PRINCESS SATAMON, THE DAUGHTER OF TEYE, RECEIVING THE GIFT OF A NECKBAND FROM TWO YOUNG GIRLS, DECORATES THE BACK OF A CHAIR (H. 17 IN, 43 CM) FOUND IN THE TOMB OF YUIA AND TUIA (EGYPTIAN MUSEUM, CAIRO).

Amenhotep IV (1350–1333 BC), the son of Amenhotep III and Queen Teye, began his reign by building a series of edifices dedicated to the god Re'-Harakhty in his guise as the sun disk (Aten) east of the Karnak enclosure. These structures were dismantled by later pharaohs, and what remains is a series of small sandstone tiles (*talatat*) decorated in relief, which were found inside Pylon IX at Karnak, and the famous colossal statues that portray the king with features that are quite unusual for ancient Egyptian iconography. In fact, the pharaoh has an elongated head, hollow cheeks, large protruding lips, a pronounced chin, rather flabby muscles and a prominent stomach. The drastic stylistic innovations in the Karnak monuments, built in the king's fifth year of rule, heralded a change of even greater significance: Amenhotep IV, accompanied by his consort Nefertiti, moved the capital of the kingdom to a city in Middle Egypt, near the present-day locality of el-Amarna, which he founded for this occasion. The new city, whose surface area was bounded by 14 landmarks, was named Akhetaten ("Horizon of Aten"). A central district, cut through by a large street that crossed the entire city, was the site of the Royal Palace, a large temple dedicated to the sun god, a small sanctuary, and some administrative offices. The southern zone of the city was occupied by a residential quarter reserved for high-ranking persons. Another area further south, where the artisans' workshops were located, yielded the famous bust of Nefertiti now on display in the Egyptian Museum, Berlin. In the northern section of the city stood a royal residence, probably the queen's, and another residential area. While the new capital was being founded Amenhotep IV changed his name to Akhenaten ("beneficial to the sun disk"), thus triggering a rupture with the official religion and the cult of the sun god Amon-Re'. Worship of the numerous gods of the Egyptian pantheon was tolerated at first, but it was soon prohibited and replaced by the exclusive cult of the sun disk Aten. The most important temples in the country were closed and the images of the gods were erased from the monuments. The highest expression of the new religious concepts found in a religious hymn, the *Hymn to Aten*, which the pharaoh himself composed and which was carved on the walls of a rock tomb at Amarna belonging to the vizier Aya, who was probably Nefertiti's father and the future pharaoh. The Amarnian religious reform also influenced the role of the king, since only Akhenaten and his family could come into contact with Aten, who was portrayed only as a sun disk whose long rays ended in hands that act as mediators between the god and humans. Therefore, the royal family became the object of a semi-divine cult and was represented in attitudes of natural intimacy on the main monuments of the time. Egyptian art was also greatly influenced by Akhenaten's profound artistic innovations: the "Amarnian style" was based on a type of realism that verged on caricature.

The end of Akhenaten's reign was marked by grief: after the death of a daughter, Nefertiti suddenly disappeared and was replaced as the principal royal consort by her daughter Merytaten. It is not certain that Nefertiti was buried in the tomb prepared for her at Amarna. Akhenaten probably named as his coregent a young and little known court personage, Smenkhare', who died a short time afterward. It may be that the mummy found in Tomb KV 55 in the Valley of the Kings, inside a sarcophagus originally prepared for Queen Teye, really belongs to this young prince who died so prematurely. Akhenaten himself died soon afterward and was perhaps buried in his rock tomb at Amarna.

114 LEFT - THE BUST OF NEFERTITI (H. 19 IN, 48 CM) COMES FROM AMARNA (EGYPTIAN MUSEUM, BERLIN).

114 RIGHT - AKHENATEN, NEFERTITI AND THEIR DAUGHTERS ADORING THE SUN DISK IN THIS TABLET FROM AMARNA (H. 21 IN, 53 CM; EGYPTIAN MUSEUM, CAIRO).

115 - THIS COLOSSUS (H. 6 FT, 1.85 M) DECORATED A TEMPLE OF AMENHOTEP IV AT KARNAK (EGYPTIAN MUSEUM, CAIRO).

The new pharaoh was the young Tutankhaten (1333–1323 BC), may be brother of Smenkhare', who married Princess Ankhesanpaten, Akhenaten's daughter. The young king, probably under the supervision of the vizier Aya and general Horemhab, changed his name to Tutankhamun and revived the traditional Egyptian religion, abandoning Amarna and making Memphis the capital of the country once again. The brief reign of Tutankhamun, who died when only eighteen, probably of natural causes, would not have gone down in history had his tomb in the Valley of the Kings (KV 62) not been discovered virtually intact, providing us with one of the most precious archaeological treasures of all time. The discovery that Howard Carter made in 1922 affords first-hand knowledge of New Kingdom mortuary regalia and allows us to admire some absolute masterpieces of ancient Egyptian art, the most outstanding examples of which are the pharaoh's throne, his parade chariot, the gilded wooden sacella, or shrines, that sealed the mortuary chamber, the three anthropoid sarcophagi or coffins that protected the mummy, and the famous gold death mask.

116 - THE GOLD MASK (H. 21 1/4 IN, 54 CM) OF TUTANKHAMUN COVERED THE MUMMY'S FACE OF THE PROTAGONIST OF THE LAST PHASE OF THE AMARNA PERIOD (EGYPTIAN MUSEUM, CAIRO).

117 - ON THE BACK OF THE THRONE OF TUTANKHAMUN (H. 3 FT 4 IN, 102 CM) IS A PORTRAIT OF THE PHARAOH BEING ANOINTED BY ANKHESENAMON (EGYPTIAN MUSEUM, CAIRO).

118

118-119 — THE WALL OF THE
BURIAL CHAMBER IN
TUTANKHAMUN'S TOMB
DEPICTS THE PHARAOH
ACCOMPANIED BY HIS KA IN
THE PRESENCE OF OSIRIS
(LEFT), THE PHARAOH
BEFORE THE GODDESS NUT
(CENTER), AND THE OPENING
OF THE MOUTH CEREMONY
OFFICIATED BY AYA.

118 BOTTOM AND 119 TOP -
EACH OF THESE USHABTI
FROM THE GRAVE GOODS
OF TUTANKHAMUN HAS
A DIFFERENT CROWN:
THE WHITE ONE OF
UPPER EGYPT, THE BLUE
ONE, THE RED ONE OF
LOWER EGYPT, AND
THE NEMES (EGYPTIAN
MUSEUM, CAIRO).

119 CENTER - INSIDE
TUTANKHAMUN'S BURIAL
CHAMBER (WHOSE BACK
WALL HAS SCENES FROM
THE *BOOK OF THE DEAD*)
THERE IS STILL THE
EXTERNAL COFFIN THAT
HOUSED THE PHARAOH'S
MUMMY.

119 BOTTOM - IN THE CACHE
OF TUTANKHAMUN, HOWARD
CARTER FOUND THIS GILDED
COFFER (H. 3 FT 11 IN, 118 CM)
SURMOUNTED BY A STATUE
OF THE JACKAL SACRED TO
ANUBIS AND RESTING ON A
SEDAN CHAIR (EGYPTIAN
MUSEUM, CAIRO).

The premature death of Tutankhamun left the throne of Egypt without an heir. Queen Ankhesenamon even went so far as to ask the Hittite king Suppiluliumas I to send a royal prince to Egypt to become the new pharaoh. But this attempt at a diplomatic marriage between the two main empires in the Near East probably failed because the elderly vizier Aya (1323–1319 BC) – already depicted on the tomb of Tutankhamun while officiating the Opening of the Mouth funerary ceremony of the dead pharaoh – ascended the throne. Aya's reign was also short-lived, and another high-ranking official in the Amarna court became pharaoh: the chief of the army Horemhab (1319–1291 BC). The new ruler promoted a policy of restoration of order in the land, which amounted to erasing all memory of Akhenaten and Amarna. Horemhab carried out a vast building program at Karnak, usurped the mortuary temple of Aya at Medinet Habu, where he erected a statue originally intended for Tu-

tankhamun, and commissioned a small rock-cut temple near Gebel el-Silsila, between Edfu and Kom Ombo. Horemhab was buried in Tomb KV 57 of the Valley of the Kings, despite the fact that, before becoming pharaoh, he had already ordered the construction of a large tomb at southern Saqqara that looked like a small temple, with an entrance pylon and two peristyle courts. The innermost part of the tomb housed three shrines for offerings, the middle of which was originally surmounted by a small pyramid, and two shafts led to the underground burial chamber. Horemhab's tomb at Saqqara has provided us with reliefs with a pronounced Amarnian influence that are now in several museums and that have different scenes, including one of the general receiving honors from Tutankhamun and another depicting a row of Asiatic and Nubian war prisoners.

120 TOP - AT THE END OF A LONG CORRIDOR THAT DESCENDS INTO THE TOMB OF HOREMHAB IN THE VALLEY OF THE KINGS IS A SHAFT CHAMBER WHOSE WALLS ARE DECORATED WITH ILLUSTRATIONS OF THE KING IN THE PRESENCE OF VARIOUS DIVINITIES.

120-121 - THE FOUR CHILDREN OF HORUS—QEBESENUF, DUAMUTEF, IMSET AND HA'PY—SEATED AT AN OFFERINGS TABLE IN THIS WALL PAINTING IN THE BURIAL CHAMBER OF AYA'S TOMB.

121 TOP - ON THE WEST WALL OF THE ANTECHAMBER OF HOREMHAB'S TOMB THE KING IS OFFERING TWO VASES OF WINE TO THE GOD HARSIESE, WHO IS WEARING THE DOUBLE CROWN OF EGYPT.

121 BOTTOM - ON THE WEST WALL OF THE ANTECHAMBER OF HOREMHAB'S TOMB THE PHARAOH IS DEPICTED BEFORE THE GOD ANUBIS AND OFFERING LIBATIONS TO THE GODDESS ISIS, WHO IS REPRESENTED WITH HATHORIC HORNS.

120 BOTTOM — THIS SCENE OF THE SECOND HOUR IN THE *BOOK OF THE GATES* WAS PAINTED ON THE ENTRANCE WALL OF HOREMHAB'S BURIAL CHAMBER. IN THE UPPER REGISTER THE BARK OF THE RAM-HEADED SOLAR GOD IS BEING PULLED BY THE DEAD PERSONS IN THE PRESENCE OF SEVEN DIVINITIES. IN THE LOWER REGISTER THE GOD ATUM, LEANING ON A STAFF, OBSERVES FOUR MEN LYING ON THEIR BACKS AND A ROW OF BOUND MEN, ALL OF WHOM HAVE BEEN JUDGED UNFIT FOR THE AFTERLIFE BY RE'.

Horemhab chose as his successor a military leader, Paramessu, who hailed from the Delta and had already served as vizier. Ascending the throne with the name of Ramesses I (1291–1289 BC), he was the first pharaoh of the 19th Dynasty but ruled for too short a period to leave any significant marks of his activity. The king's mummy, originally buried in a small tomb in the Valley of the Kings (KV 16), was recently identified and transferred from the United States, where it had been kept, to the Egyptian Museum, Cairo. His successor Sethos I (1289–1279 ca.) resumed military activity in the Near East, which had been interrupted during the Amarna period. Taking advantage of the domestic problems assailing the Egyptian state, the Hittite Empire gained control of the Palestinian coast by means of a system of alliances. The military campaigns of Sethos I, through which Egypt extended its supremacy as far as the Syrian city of Qadesh, were represented on the outer north wall of the great hypostyle hall in the Temple of Karnak, work on which was begun by Sethos himself. However, Sethos I's architectural masterpiece is the sanctuary he built at Abydos, the city sacred to the god of the Afterlife, Osiris. The temple, dedicated to the principal Egyptian divinities and to the funerary cult of the pharaoh, has an unusual L-shaped layout. The section that has been preserved includes the portico of the second court, decorated with scenes com-

missioned by Ramesses II, behind which are aligned two hypostyle halls with splendid painted relief carving dating from the period of Sethos I. At the end of the second hypostyle hall are seven chapels dedicated to the cult of Sethos I, Ptah, Re'-Harakhty, Amon-Re', Osiris, Isis and Horus. The chapel of Osiris affords access to another set of rooms at the back of the temple dedicated to the Osiris–Isis–Horus triad. The south end of the temple was occupied by storerooms, a hall dedicated to the Memphite gods Ptah-Sokar and Nefertum, and a long gallery that once contained a king list (now in the Louvre, Paris) with the names of the Egyptian pharaohs. Behind the temple, Sethos built a cenotaph (Osireion) for the god of the Afterlife, Osiris. This underground edifice, accessible by a long, sloping corridor decorated with funerary texts, was a large hall supported by ten pillars, in the middle of which was a stone island surrounded by water and bearing the sarcophagus and canopic jars of the god. In the back was a room in the shape of a sarcophagus with relief carvings of astronomical motifs. The mortuary temple that Sethos I built on the west bank of Thebes, at the locality of Qurna, has been only partly preserved, while his tomb (KV 17) in the Valley of the Kings is one of the largest and most beautiful in the entire necropolis, with elegant painted decoration and a fine set of funerary texts.

122 - THIS ALABASTER STATUE OF SETHOS I (H. 7 FT 9 IN, 2.38 M) FOUND IN THE CACHE AT KARNAK ONCE HAD INLAY AND A CROWN MADE OF A DIFFERENT MATERIAL (EGYPTIAN MUSEUM, CAIRO).

123 - THE SOLAR BARK PASSES THROUGH THE THIRD HOUR OF THE BOOK OF THE GATES WHILE THE GOD ATUM DRIVES AWAY THE SERPENT APOPIS IN THE TOMB OF RAMESSES I.

124 - PROFILE OF SETHOS I, WHO IS WEARING THE *NEMES* AND THE ROYAL URAEUS AND HAS A FALSE BEARD, ON ONE OF THE COLUMNS IN THE BURIAL CHAMBER OF HIS TOMB IN THE VALLEY OF THE KINGS.

125 TOP - A REPRESENTATION OF THE NOCTURNAL CONSTELLATIONS DECORATES THIS PART OF THE VAULT IN THE LOWER SECTION OF SETHOS I'S BURIAL CHAMBER.

125 CENTER - THE COLORS OF THIS WALL IN THE ANTECHAMBER OF SETHOS I'S TOMB, ON WHICH THE PHARAOH IS DEPICTED IN THE PRESENCE OF VARIOUS DIVINITIES, WERE RUINED BY THE MOLDS MADE OF THEM IN THE 19TH CENTURY.

125 BOTTOM - THE SHORT WALLS IN THE LOWER SECTION OF SETHOS I'S BURIAL CHAMBER HAVE PORTRAYALS OF THE GODDESSES ISIS AND NEPHTHYS WITH OUTSPREAD WINGS; BELOW THEM ARE THE TEXTS AND ILLUSTRATIONS OF THE FIRST HOURS OF THE NIGHT IN THE *BOOK OF THE DEAD*.

126 TOP - SETHOS I OFFERS
INCENSE TO ISIS IN THIS
RELIEF ON A WALL IN THE
SECOND HYPOSTYLE HALL OF
THE TEMPLE AT ABYDOS.

126 BOTTOM - SETHOS I
BUILT HIS MORTUARY TEMPLE
AT THE LOCATLITY OF
QURNA, ON THE WEST BANK
OF THEBES. THE ONLY

REMAINING PART IS THE
INNERMOST SECTION,
PRECEDED BY A TEN-
COLUMN PORTICO.

127 - THE FIRST HYPOSTYLE
HALL IN THE TEMPLE OF
SETHOS I AT ABYDOS
STILL HAS SOME OF THE
ORIGINAL COLORS ON THE
COLUMNS.

The son of Sethos I, Ramesses II (1279–1212 BC), is perhaps the best-known pharaoh in Egyptian history because of the great number of monuments he erected and had named after himself. His long reign marked a period of prosperity and development for Egypt and in fact the fame of this pharaoh spread well beyond the country's borders. Despite this, the beginning of Ramesses II's reign was marked by conflict as the struggle against the Hittite Empire continued, albeit in a latent manner. In his fifth year of rule the Egyptian and Hittite armies fought a battle near the city of Qadesh that was immortalized on the walls of sev-

eral temples as a major military success by Ramesses II despite the fact that the outcome was anything but decisive. The pylons and outer walls of the temple of Luxor, the walls in the great hypostyle hall at Karnak, the outer walls of the temple of Abydos, and the pylons of the Ramesseum were all used by the pharaoh to have himself represented triumphant on his war chariot against his enemies, even though in reality the battle came within an inch of being a disastrous rout for the Egyptians. The long dispute with the Hittite Empire ended in Ramesses II's twentieth year of rule, when the two nations signed a peace treaty that was cemented by a diplomatic marriage between Ramesses II and a Hittite princess. Ramesses II also carried out military campaigns in the south, in Nubia, where he had to quell revolts. But the pharaoh was active in Nubia most of all as a builder, as attested by the seven temples he constructed there, many of which are rock-hewn. He had small rock temples

built at Beit el-Wali and el-Derr, while the sanctuary of the god Ptah at Gerf Hussein was only partly rock-hewn. A particularly important monument because of its size was the temple of el-Sebu'a: access to the sanctuary was gained through two forecourts preceded by two pylons and flanked by two rows of human-headed and ram-headed sphinxes. A third pylon, decorated with colossi of the king, led to a peristyle court with Osiride pillars on whose walls was a long row of Ramesses II's children.

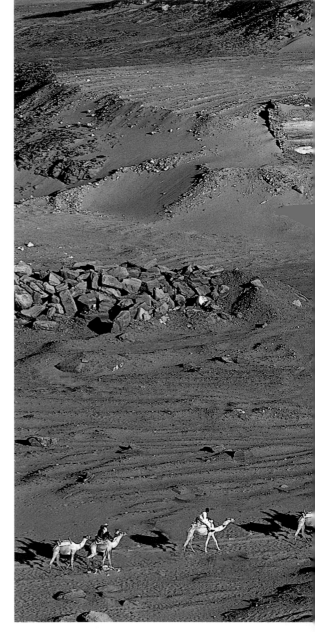

The rock-cut sanctuary was made up of a hypostyle hall with 12 pillars and three chapels containing the sacred barks and the divine statues. But the real architectural masterpieces of Ramesses II in Nubia are the two sanctuaries hewn out of the rock at Abu Simbel, which in the 1960s were dismantled and placed in a more elevated position in order to save them from the waters of Lake Nasser, which would have submerged them after the construction of the Aswan High Dam.

128 TOP - THE SECOND ATRIUM IN THE ROCK-HEWN NUBIAN TEMPLE BUILT FOR RAMESSES II AT EL-DERR IN HONOR OF AMON-RE' AND RE'-HARAKHTY IS SUPPORTED BY SIX PILLARS AND DECORATED WITH RELIGIOUS SCENES.

128 BOTTOM - THE ENTRANCE OF THE TEMPLE OF WADI EL-SEBU'A WAS FLANKED BY TWO STATUES OF RAMESSES II WEARING THE DOUBLE CROWN.

128-129 - THE PARTLY ROCK-HEWN TEMPLE BUILT BY RAMESSES II AT WADI EL-SEBU'A HAS NUMEROUS HUMAN- AND FALCON-HEADED SPHINXES. UNFORTUNATELY, ONLY THE THIRD PYLON OF THIS EDIFICE HAS REMAINED.

129 – THIS STATUE (H. 2 FT 7 IN, 80 CM) FROM TANIS PORTRAYS RAMESSES II WITH A SHORT WIG AND PLEATED GARB (EGYPTIAN MUSEUM, CAIRO).

The Great Temple of Abu Simbel has a monumental façade whose shape reminds one of a temple pylon, from which there emerge four colossal statues of the enthroned Ramesses II. At the foot of the colossi, carved on a much smaller scale, are statues of the members of the royal family – the pharaoh's mother Muttuya, his wife Nefertari, and his sons and daughters. Above the entrance gate an iconographic cryptogram conceals the pharaoh's "throne name": the sun god Re' (with a falcon's head) is holding a scepter (*user*) and a figurine of the goddess Ma'at (*Userma'atre'*). The upper part of the façade is bordered by a row of baboons, animals sacred to the god of writing, Thoth. In the interior, the first hypostyle hall is supported by eight pillars with Osirian statues of the pharaoh. Some secondary chambers, probably used as storerooms, open onto the hypostyle hall, on whose walls are scenes carved in relief depicting the Battle of Qadesh. The

second hypostyle hall is supported by four pillars with a square plinth that are decorated with cult scenes. A transverse vestibule gives access to the sanctuary, made up of three chapels. In the middle chapel stood the statues of the four gods venerated in this temple: Ptah, Re'-Harakhty, Amon-Re' and the deified Ramesses. Next to the Great Temple, Ramesses II built another rock-cut temple, known as the Small Temple, dedicated to Queen Nefertari and the goddess Hathor. Six colossal statues, four of Ramesses II and two of Nefertari wearing a Hathoric crown, are interspersed by buttresses, all of which go to make up the temple façade. The interior consists of a single hypostyle hall with six pillars on which is represented a large Hathoric sistrum, and a chapel in the back in which a statue of the goddess-cow Hathor emerges from the rock, protecting Ramesses II.

130 LEFT - THE CARTOUCHES ON THE GREAT TEMPLE OF ABU SIMBEL BEAR THE NAMES OF RAMESSES II.

130 RIGHT - THE FAÇADE OF THE SMALL TEMPLE AT ABU SIMBEL HAS SIX NICHES WITH STATUES OF THE KING AND QUEEN.

130-131 - FOUR COLOSSAL STATUES OF RAMESSES II ON HIS THRONE ARE ON THE FAÇADE OF THE GREAT TEMPLE OF ABU SIMBEL.

132 - THE FIRST ATRIUM OF
THE GREAT TEMPLE OF ABU
SIMBEL IS SUPPORTED BY
EIGHT OSIRIAN PILLARS
AND ITS CEILING IS
DECORATED WITH VULTURES
WITH OUTSPREAD WINGS
PROTECTING THE
CARTOUCHES OF
RAMESSES II.

133 - THE SECOND ATRIUM
OF THE GREAT TEMPLE AT
ABU SIMBEL IS DECORATED
WITH RELIGIOUS SCENES. AT
THE END OF THE TEMPLE
CELLA IS A SCULPTURE
GROUP PORTRAYING THE
GODS PTAH, AMUN-RE',
RE'-HARAKHTY AND
RAMESSES II.

134-135 — THE LARGE
SCENE DEPICTING THE
MAJOR EVENTS IN THE
BATTLE OF QADESH, WHICH
RAMESSES II FOUGHT
AGAINST THE HITTITES,
IS CARVED ON THE NORTH
WALL OF THE FIRST ATRIUM
IN THE GREAT TEMPLE OF
ABU SIMBEL.

Ramesses II carried out numerous building programs in Egypt: a small temple at Abydos, to the north of the one constructed by his father; the large hypostyle hall in the Temple of Karnak; the enlargement of the Temple of Luxor; and the construction of his own mortuary temple. Ramesses II was also active in the Delta, where he founded a new capital, Pi-Ri'amsese, situated near the ancient Hyksos capital of

throne flanked the entrance to the hypostyle hall. The head of one of the two is still lying *in situ*, while a part of the second head was transported to the British Museum in London by Giovan Battista Belzoni in 1816. In the first court were found a statue of the pharaoh (identified as the "Sun of Princes") at least 52 ft (16 m) high, whose fragments are now scattered all over the ground, and a statue of the queen mother, Tuya.

Avaris. At Memphis the king erected several monuments that contained, among other things, the two famous colossi of the pharaoh, one lying at the site of Mit Rahina and the other recently transferred from the central railway station square in Cairo to Giza.

The pharaoh's mortuary temple (Ramesseum), built on the west bank of Thebes, consisted of two entrance pylons, two pillared courts, a hypostyle hall and the inner sanctuary. The complex was completed by a small palace facing the first court by means of a "Window of Appearance," and a sanctuary dedicated to Ramesses II's mother Tuya. The pillars that once supported the portico in the second court were decorated with Osiride colossi of Ramesses II and, again in the second court, two stone colossi of the pharaoh seated on his

The structures surrounding the main temple on three sides are particularly impressive: they consist of a series of storerooms, granaries, administrative offices, stables, spaces used as abattoirs, and kitchens, all of which were used for the temple activities and cult rituals, as well as for the economic life of the urban community. The large tomb (KV 7) prepared for the pharaoh in the Valley of the Kings was seriously damaged over the centuries, while that of Queen Nefertari, hewn out of the rock in the Valley of the Queens (QV 66), still has magnificent wall paintings. As the last resting place of the many children he had had during his long reign, Ramesses II had the largest tomb in the Valley of the Kings (KV 5) — articulated on several levels and with a long set of rooms, pillared halls, corridors and chapels — cut out of the living rock.

136 - IN THE FIRST COURT OF THE TEMPLE OF LUXOR, NEAR THE ENTRANCE OF THE COLUMNED CORRIDOR, IS A COLOSSUS OF RAMESSES II SEATED ON HIS THRONE.

137 TOP LEFT - AT THE END OF THE SECOND COURT OF THE RAMESSEUM ARE SOME PILLARS DECORATED WITH OSIRIAN STATUES.

137 TOP RIGHT - AERIAL VIEW OF THE RUINS OF THE RAMESSEUM.

137 BOTTOM - THE UPPER REGISTER OF THE RELIEF ON THE PORTICO OF THE SECOND COURT OF THE RAMESSEUM ILLUSTRATES RAMESSES II MAKING OFFERINGS TO VARIOUS GODS, WHILE IN THE LOWER REGISTER THE KING IS BEING LED BEFORE THE THEBAN TRIAD.

138 - Queen Nefertari, whose name means "the most beautiful," is depicted in her tomb in the Valley of the Queens wearing the crown in the shape of a vulture typical of Egyptian queens.

139 top - The burial chamber of Queen Nefertari has magnificent decoration that covers both the side walls and the four central pillars, while the ceiling is painted to resemble the star-studded sky.

139 bottom - This scene, which accompanies Chapter 17 of the Book of the Dead and is represented in the antechamber of the tomb of Nefertari, depicts a kiosk. Flanking the mummy are the goddesses Isis and Nephthys in the guise of falcons, the grey heron sacred to Heliopolis, and a Nilotic divinity

Ramesses II died after 67 years of rule, and was succeeded by his thirteenth son, Merneptah (1212–1202 BC), who was already rather old. The new pharaoh was called upon to defend the Egyptian borders from an invasion by Mediterranean populations (the so-called Sea Peoples) who were threatening the entire Near East. A stele erected in Merneptah's mortuary temple celebrates his victory against the enemies of Egypt and, for the first time in the country's history, mentions the population of Israel. As a builder, Merneptah was particularly active at Memphis, where he erected a small column to commemorate his military exploits and where he built a palace. His death triggered a grave dynastic crisis that weakened the reigns of the rivals Amenmesse (1202–1199 BC) and Sethos II (1199–1193 BC) and then of the young Siptah (1193–1187 BC), whose power was really exerted by his stepmother, Queen Twosre (1193–1185 BC). In any case, the queen – and hence the policies of the kingdom – seem to have been greatly influenced by Bay, a high official who may have been of Syrian origin, who was the power behind the throne and who is described in Egyptian documents as a dangerous and treacherous figure. When the young Siptah died prematurely, Twosre had herself proclaimed pharaoh and ruled the country alone until her death, which marked the end of the 19th Dynasty.

140 - THIS BUST WITH IDEALIZED FEATURES (H. 3 FT, 91 CM) BELONGED TO A STATUE OF THE SEATED MERNEPTAH THAT WAS FOUND IN THIS KING'S MORTUARY TEMPLE (EGYPTIAN MUSEUM, CAIRO).

141 LEFT - ONE OF THE NAMES USED FOR MERNEPTAH WAS "THE RAM SACRED TO RE', BELOVED BY AMON."

141 RIGHT - AT THE ENTRANCE TO THE CORRIDOR LEADING TO THE TOMB OF MERNEPTAH IN THE VALLEY OF THE KINGS IS THIS SCENE OF THE PHARAOH IN THE PRESENCE OF THE GOD RE'-HARAKHTY.

THE RAMESSID PERIOD

After Twosre died, Sethnakhte (1185–1184 BC) managed to proclaim himself pharaoh. He became the founder of the 20th Dynasty, usurped the queen's tomb (KV 14), and put an end to the period of political instability, presenting himself as the restorer of order. The son of Sethnakhte, Ramesses III (1184–1153 BC), was the last great pharaoh of the New Kingdom. He had to face new pressure, both from Libyan tribes that were invading the Delta and threats of invasions by the Sea Peoples, who in the meantime had brought about the downfall of the Hittite Empire. The pharaoh's military victories were celebrated on the walls of his mortuary temple at Medinet Habu, the best preserved of the "temples of millions of years". Inside the sacred precinct, Ramesses III incorporated a small sanctuary dedicated to Amun that had been built by Hatshepsut and Tuthmosis III and was later enlarged by the pharaohs of the Late Period and the Ptolemaic kings. The main entrance to the sacred enclosure, on the east side, was a portal that was flanked by two crenellated towers modeled after the typical Syrian fort (*migdol*) and faced the quay and canal. The first pylon of the temple – on whose façade the king was depicted defeating his enemies before the gods Amun and Re'-Harakhty – led to a court with Osiride statues of the pharaoh on the portico pillars; to the west of the court was a

royal palace with a typical Window of Appearances. A second pylon gave access to another porticoed court, on whose walls were scenes connected to the cult of Min and the procession of the sacred barks. The innermost part of the temple consisted of three hypostyle halls flanked by chapels and subsidiary rooms with relief carvings and statues of the gods, and the entire complex was surrounded by storerooms, workshops and the priest's residences. The final years of Ramesses III's rule seem to have been marked by troubling episodes and economic difficulty: a conspiracy known as the Harem Plot was organized by the pharaoh's wife Tiye and other exponents of the royal harem, with the aim of assassinating the king and replacing him with the young Pentauret, the queen's son. The conspiracy was thwarted and those responsible for it were condemned to death, but Ramesses III probably died while the trial was in progress. The pharaoh was buried in Tomb KV 11 of the Valley of the Kings, known as the Tomb of the Harpists because of the unusual and beautiful relief sculpture of two blind harpists on its walls. The Valley of the Queens has the tombs of various queens and princes of Ramesses III, only a few of which have preserved their original decoration, such as those of Queen Tity (QV 52), princes Amunherkhopshef (QV 55) and Khaemwaset (QV 44).

142 - A SCENE IN THE TOMB IN THE VALLEY OF THE KINGS THAT BELONGED TO RAMESSES III SHOWING THE PHARAOH OFFERING INCENSE TO THE GOD ATUM, WHO IS STANDING IN FRONT OF HIM.

143 - RAMESSES III HOLDING HANDS WITH GODDESS ISIS IN AN ILLUSTRATION ON ONE WALL OF THE TOMB OF AMUNHERKHOPSHEF, THE SON OF THE 20TH-DYNASTY PHARAOH.

144 - On a wall of the *migdol* in the temple of Medinet Habu is this depiction of Ramesses III defeating his Asiatic enemies in the presence of the god Re'-Harakhty.

145 top - Only the plinths of the columns in the first hypostyle hall of the temple at Medinet Habu have survived. In the background is the chapel dedicated to the god Ptah.

145 bottom - The complex of Medinet Habu, which in ancient times was called Djeme, was surrounded by a brick wall and included a royal palace, storerooms and dwellings for the priests. Opposite the entrance pylon was a small 18th-Dynasty temple, the chapels of the Divine Adoratrices, built in the Late Period, and the *migdol*.

After the death of Ramesses III, in the space of about 80 years (1153–1075 BC), there were eight other Egyptian pharaohs who called themselves Ramesses, an obvious homage to their illustrious 19th-Dynasty predecessor. This was yet another period of crisis for Egypt, marked by financial scandals, economic crises, corruption, strikes, and theft and violation that did not even spare the royal necropolises. The kings were weak and ephemeral figures and their reigns were short-lived, facts that favored the rise of the priests of Amun, whose power increased, especially around Thebes, the home of this god's powerful high priest. This grave political crisis exploded during

146-147 - THE CEILING OF RAMESSES VI'S BURIAL CHAMBER IS DECORATED WITH THE *BOOKS OF THE DAY AND NIGHT.*

147 CENTER LEFT - RAMESSES IX MAKES AN OFFERING TO THE RAM-HEADED SUN GOD IN A SCENE OF THE *BOOK OF THE CAVERNS.*

147 CENTER RIGHT - IN RAMESSES VI'S BURIAL CHAMBER THE "DESTROYER" GODDESS RISES UP TO THE SUN.

147 BELOW - RAMESSE VI'S TOMB CONTAINS SCENES FROM THE *BOOK OF THE GATES* AND THE *BOOK OF THE CAVERNS.*

the reign of Ramesses XI, the last pharaoh of the 20th Dynasty, and indeed of the New Kingdom. The country was ravaged by a civil war whose main protagonists were Herihor, the High Priest of Amun, a Nubian general called Panehsy, and the pharaoh himself. The unity of central political power was by then compromised and Egypt was split into regions that were virtually sovereign nations. In the north, Ramesses XI was the formal ruler, but true power lay in the hands of the court official Smendes, the future pharaoh and founder of the 21st Dynasty; the Thebes area was governed by the priests of Amun; and in Nubia Panehsy had established an independent state. Thus the New Kingdom came to an end in this climate of political anarchy and disorder.

THE CITY OF AMUN: THE TEMPLES OF LUXOR AND KARNAK

148-149 - THE TEMPLE OF AMUN'S ENCLOSURE AT KARNAK INCLUDED A SACRED LAKE, THE TEMPLE OF KHONS AND MANY OTHER RELIGIOUS EDIFICES.

148 BOTTOM - THIS STATUE OF THE GOD AMON WAS PROBABLY ERECTED BY TUTANKHAMUN IN THE COURT OF THE SIXTH PYLON IN THE TEMPLE OF KARNAK.

149 TOP - THE RAM-HEADED SPHINXES THAT PRECEDE THE FIRST PYLON OF THE TEMPLE AT KARNAK HOLD THE OSIRIAN FIGURE OF RAMESSES II IN THEIR PAWS.

149 BOTTOM - IN FRONT OF THE SECOND PYLON OF THE TEMPLE OF KARNAK IS A COLOSSAL STATUE OF RAMESSES II.

west for the dead and their funerary cult — were dotted with stone temples and edifices whose ruins have been preserved. The main "beneficiary" of the enterprising building programs of the New Kingdom pharaohs was the local god Amun, in the syncretic guise of Amun-Re', in honor of whom the most important sanctuaries in ancient Egypt were erected.

The center of the Amun cult was the sanctuary of Karnak, which was founded in the Middle Kingdom but totally rebuilt and continuously enlarged by the New Kingdom kings, who turned it into the largest temple in Egypt. The Great Temple of Amun at Karnak was laid out along two axes, the main axis with an east–west alignment and the secondary axis perpendicular to it. The temple was surrounded by numerous secondary edifices, as well by the sanctuaries dedicated to the goddess Mut, Amun's wife, their son Khons, and the ancient Theban god Montu.

Tuthmosis I built two pylons (IV and V) in front of the sanctuary for the sacred bark and in the enclosed space between the two he built a hypostyle hall. In front of the entrance pylon the pharaoh erected two obelisks, one of which still exists. Later on, Queen Hatshepsut built a shrine for the sacred bark (the so-called Red Chapel) next to the main temple and added two obelisks inside the hypostyle hall of Tuthmosis I. It was probably during her reign that a pylon (VIII) was constructed along the processional avenue that led to the temple of the goddess Mut, to the south of the main precinct, faced by colossal statues of the queen, her predecessors and Tuthmosis III. This latter promoted drastic changes in the layout of the temple, building a new, small pylon (VI) in front the sacred bark shrine, decorating the side walls with the *Annals of Tuthomosis III* which described his military campaigns, and erecting two stone pylons with relief sculptures of the plants that symbolize Egypt – papyrus and lotus. Behind the sanctuary, Tuthmosis III constructed a large festival temple (*Akhmenu*) that is perpendicular to the main alignment of the temple. This edifice included a large hall divided into three aisles, the side aisles supported by pillars and the central one by columns shaped like the form of the poles of a tent; a set of chapels and storerooms, including a hall ("botanical garden") decorated with detailed renderings of flora and fauna. With the building of Pylon VII the pharaoh inaugurated the secondary alignment of the temple, which had a north-south orientation.

Amenhotep III built two new pylons: Pylon III along the main axis and Pylon X, made of brick, which terminated the secondary axis to the south and was later replaced by a stone

During the New Kingdom, Thebes became a great metropolis and the favorite "showroom" of the pharaohs' grand architectural achievements. What had been a simple provincial capital was transformed into a great monumental center, where the most important pharaohs vied with one another to commemorate their respective reigns and exploits. The two banks of the Nile — the east reserved for the living and the

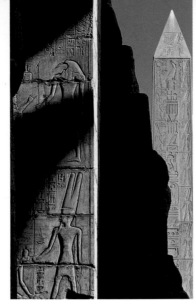

pylon erected by Horemheb. The last pharaoh of the 18th Dynasty completed the secondary axis of the temple with the placement of a new pylon (IX) along the avenue that led to the Temple of Mut. A festival edifice built by Amenhotep II is in the court that was created by the pylon. In the temple of the goddess Mut, Amenhotep III placed hundreds of statues of the lioness goddess Sakhmet; they are now on exhibit in several major museums throughout the world.

After the brief period of the Amarna reform, Horemhab began the construction of Pylon II, which was finished by the first pharaohs of the 19th Dynasty (Sethos I and Ramesses II), who also built the grand hypostyle hall behind it. This latter, vast space is occupied by a forest of 134 monumental papyrus columns that are separated by a central corridor supported by 12 larger columns with papyrus bundle capitals whose surfaces are entirely covered with reliefs and inscriptions. The in-

ner walls of the hall have relief decoration with ritual scenes, while on the outside Sethos I and Ramesses II decided to have their military campaigns in Asia illustrated. In the court opposite Pylon II, Ramesses II placed an avenue of ram-headed sphinxes, Sethos II constructed a tripartite shrine for the sacred barks, and Ramesses III built a small temple perpendicular to the court, with scenes illustrating the procession of the sacred barks and Osiride pillars. Construction of the Temple of Amun was finished in the Late Period. Sheshonq I (22nd Dynasty) decorated the first court with two lateral colonnades, while the Kushite ruler Taharqa (Late Period) erected a kiosk with papyrus bundle capitals in the middle of the court. Pylon I of the temple, which was never finished, dates from the 30th Dynasty and is preceded by an avenue of sphinxes laid out by Ramesses II and usurped by the High Priest of Amun, Pinudjem, in the 21st Dynasty.

150 - THE VAST HYPOSTYLE HALL IN THE TEMPLE OF KARNAK, WHICH WAS BUILT DURING THE REIGNS OF SETHOS I AND RAMESSES II, HAS A CENTRAL AXIS WITH 12 PAPYRUS BUNDLE COLUMNS THAT ARE 75 FT (23 M) HIGH.

151 TOP LEFT - THE LARGE COLUMNS IN THE HYPOSTYLE HALL WERE COVERED WITH RELIEF DECORATION.

151 TOP RIGHT - ONE OF THE OBELISKS ERECTED BY QUEEN HATSHEPSUT AT KARNAK RISES UP BETWEEN THE FOURTH AND FIFTH PYLON.

151 BOTTOM - THE 122 SIDE COLUMNS IN THE HYPOSTYLE HALL AT KARNAK HAVE A CIRCUMFERENCE OF OVER 26 FT (8 M) AND ARE 50 FT (15 M) HIGH.

The Great Temple of Amun at Karnak was closely linked to the sanctuary of Luxor (the so-called south harem). Once a year, on the occasion of the Festival of Opet, a religious procession with the sacred barks and the effigies of the gods Amun, Mut and Khonsu went from the former to the latter. The Luxor temple was used to worship the syncretic form of Amun-Min, who in his ithyphallic guise was connected to rebirth and regeneration. Two pharaohs in particular are to be credited with the construction of the temple: Amenhotep III and Ramesses II. The former built the inner part, which consists of a sanctuary, four antechambers with columns, and some secondary chambers. In front of these was a hypostyle hall connected to a large court with porticoes on three sides supported by a double row of lotus bundle columns. The entrance to the Temple of Amenhotep III consisted of a long processional colonnade with 14 papyrus bundle columns. The walls that surrounded the colonnade were decorated during the reigns of Tutankhamun and Horemhab, with reliefs depicting scenes of the Festival of Opet. Opposite the processional colonnade Ramesses II built a peristyle court with a double row of columns on all four sides whose alignment does not correspond to the main axis of the temple. This was probably because the court was built around a small temple dedicated to the Amun triad that dated from the reign of Hatshepsut. Placed among the 74 papyrus columns in the peristyle are colossal standing statues of Ramesses II and Amenhotep III. In front of the temple Ramesses II erected an entrance pylon decorated with scenes of the Battle of Qadesh flanked by colossal statues of himself. Only one of the two obelisks that originally framed the entranceway is still in place; the other is now in Paris. Fronting the entrance pylon, an avenue of human-headed sphinxes – the work of Nectanebo I – linked the Luxor temple with the temple complex of Karnak.

152 LEFT - RAMESSES II ERECTED COLOSSAL STATUES IN THE AREA BETWEEN THE COLUMNS IN THE FIRST COURT OF THE TEMPLE OF LUXOR, SOME OF WHICH WERE USURPED BY AMENHOTEP IIII.

152 RIGHT - THIS AERIAL VIEW SHOWS HOW THE FIRST COURT OF THE TEMPLE OF LUXOR IS NOT ALIGNED WITH THE INNERMOST PART OF THE SANCTUARY, BECAUSE RAMESSES II INCORPORATED A MORE ANCIENT CHAPEL THEREIN.

153 - IN FRONT OF THE ENTRANCE PYLON OF THE TEMPLE OF LUXOR RAMESSES II ERECTED TWO OBELISKS (ONE OF WHICH IS NOW IN PARIS) AND TWO COLOSSAL STATUES OF HIMSELF SEATED ON HIS THRONE.

The New Kingdom marked a profound change in royal funerary architecture, since the pyramid and its funerary complex were abandoned. The function of the valley temple was replaced in the New Kingdom by the "temple of millions of years," a true sanctuary that was erected to celebrate the cult of the deceased pharaoh, situated at the edge of the alluvial plain of the west bank of Thebes. However, the so-called temples of millions of years were not only intended for the funerary cult but were also places where the dynastic god Amun-Re' was worshipped, as well as being venues of economic activity. In fact, the temples were often part of religious processions during the main festivals connected to the cult of Amun. In particular, during the Beautiful

system of redistribution, could pay the salaries and bonuses of the workmen, artisans, officials and military men. Even the pharaoh, who on special occasions would manifest himself in the "window of appearances" situated in the first court of the mortuary temple, could recompense his most faithful offices with prizes and riches. The true innovation in the royal burial during the New Kingdom was that almost all the pharaohs in this period had themselves interred in tombs cut out of the desert wadis in the Theban hills. Sixty-three tombs were rock-cut in the Valley of the Kings, the last one being discovered in February 2006 near the tomb of Tutankhamun, containing a deposit of embalming material. The walls of the royal tombs were decorated with new-

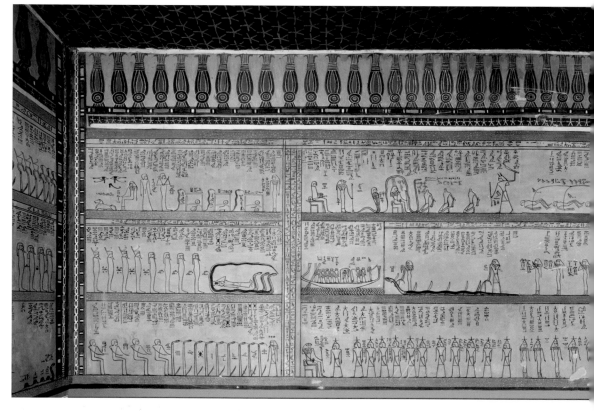

Feast of the Valley, the sacred barks that transported the statues of the Theban triad of Amun, Mut and Khonsu went from Karnak on the other bank of the Nile toward the mortuary temples of Deir el-Bahri and from there proceeded to the mortuary temple of the reigning pharaoh. Furthermore, the temples also possessed farmland, livestock and a host of other riches, and the products belonging to the temple were gathered and then processed in the structures surrounding the sanctuaries. The temple was an actual economic institution which, by means of a

ly composed funerary texts, the most ancient of which, known as Am Duat ("that which is found in the Afterlife"), narrates the journey made by the sun bark during the 12 nocturnal hours through the Underworld. In the sixth hour of this journey the soul (ba) of the dead pharaoh merges with the sun to complete the journey that will take him to the rebirth of the morning. The text of the Am Duat decorates the walls of the burial chamber of Tuthmosis III and Amenhotep II and part of the walls in other kings' tombs. The Litany of Re', a collection of invocations to the

sun god, with whom the deceased pharaoh was associated, was placed in the first corridors of the tomb in the Ramessid period. *The Book of the Celestial Cow*, which accompanied a portrait of the cow goddess Hathor, narrated the rebellion of humanity against the sun god Re' and the destructive revenge of the goddess, who was placated only thanks to an inebriant; the book was reproduced in the halls adjacent to the burial chamber in the tombs of Sethos I, and Ramesses II and III. The book of *Am Duat* gave rise to the *Book of the Gates*, which deals with the journey of the solar bark in the nocturnal Underworld in 12 hours that are separated from one another by gates. This text was carved for the first time in the tomb of Horemhab and then during the

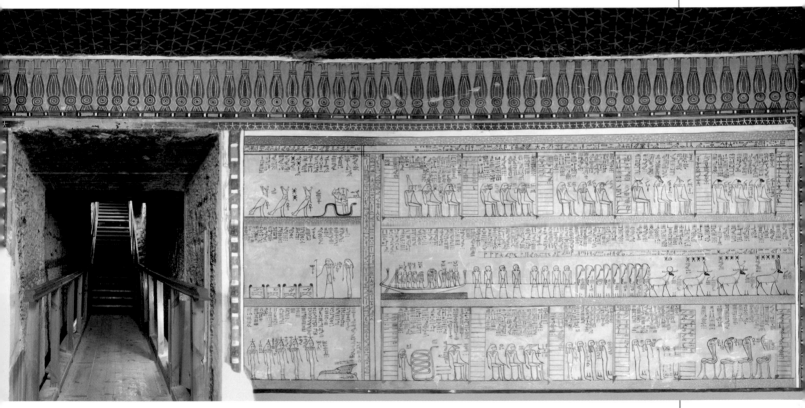

Ramessid period, and appears in its unabridged version in the tomb of Ramesses VI. *The Book of the Caverns*, present in the tombs of Merneptah, Twosre and Ramesses III and VI, depicts the Afterlife studded with caves containing the souls of the dead. From the reign of Ramesses IV on, the star-studded sky formally illustrated on the tomb ceilings was replaced by representations of the celestial goddess Nut who swallows the solar disk at night and gives birth to it from her body at dawn (*The Book of Nut* and *The Book of Night*).

154-155 - ON THE WALLS OF THE ENTRANCE TO THE BURIAL CHAMBER IN AMENHOTEP II'S TOMB, ON THREE REGISTERS, ARE THE TEXTS AND ILLUSTRATIONS OF THE SIXTH, SEVENTH AND EIGHTH HOURS OF THE *BOOK OF THE DEAD*.

155 TOP - A SCENE FROM THE TOMB OF TUTANKHAMUN REPRESENTING THE SOLAR BARK TRANSPORTING THE SUN IN THE GUISE OF A SCARAB (*KHEPRI*) THROUGH SIX HOURS OF THE NIGHT REPRESENTED BY SIX BABOONS.

155 BOTTOM - DETAIL FROM THE TWELFTH HOUR IN THE *BOOK OF THE DEAD* ILLUSTRATED IN THE TOMB OF AMENHOTEP II.

156 LEFT AND RIGHT - THESE
DETAILS OF THE SEVENTH HOUR
IN THE *BOOK OF THE DEAD* ARE
PART OF THE DECORATION IN
RAMESSES VI'S TOMB.

156-157 TOP - SCENE OF THE
NINTH HOUR OF *BOOK OF THE
GATES* IN THE TOMB OF
TWOSRE AND SETHNAKHTE.

156-157 BOTTOM - THE TEXT
OF THE THIRD HOUR OF
THE *BOOK OF THE DEAD*,
ILLUSTRATED IN THE TOMB
OF SETHOS I IN THE VALLLEY
OF THE KINGS, CONTAINS A
SCENE REPRESENTING A ROW
OF BOATS ACCOMPANYING THE
SOLAR BARK INTO THE
AFTERLIFE.

WEST THEBES:
THE TOMBS OF THE OFFICIALS

Our knowledge of the New Kingdom derives not only from the royal tombs, but also from the precious documentation provided in the private sepulchers. Many of these, cut out of the rock on the hills that border the west bank near Luxor, belonged to high-ranking officials who were active in Thebes in the 18th, 19th and 20th dynasties. This range of hills has various necropolises that offer a vivid description of the daily life and funerary beliefs in Thebes during the New Kingdom.

In the necropolis of Qurnet Mura'i, situated behind the mortuary temple of Amenhotep III, is the tomb of Amenhotep, known as Huy (TT 40), the viceroy of Nubia during the reign of Tutankhamun. This tomb, which was entered through an outer court, has a simple layout consisting of a long transverse cor-

ridor and a small square hall with four pillars and a niche at the end. The wall painting in the corridor has interesting scenes depicting the arrival of the ships at Thebes and the procession of the Nubian princes and their tributes to the pharaoh, the return of Huy and his family in a boat from Nubia, and the investiture of the dignitary by the pharaoh.

Between Qurnet Mura'i and the site of Deir el-Bahri lies the private necropolis of Sheikh 'Abd el-Qurna, situated behind the Ramesseum. It has hundreds of tombs, mostly dating from the 18th Dynasty, some of which boast absolute masterpieces of painting decoration.

The tomb of Rekhmire' (TT 100), the vizier during the reigns of Tuthmosis III and Amenhotep II, has a transverse hall

158-159 - THE VIZIER REKHMIRE', IN THIS SCENE IN HIS TOMB, IS SUPERVISING VARIOUS ACTIVITIES CONNECTED WITH FOOD PRODUCTION.

158 BOTTOM LEFT - TWO NUBIANS BRING A GIRAFFE TO THE VIZIER REKHMIRE', IN A SCENE IN HIS TOMB.

and another hall consisting of a long, narrow corridor perpendicular to the first one. The numerous scenes decorating the walls of this tomb illustrate the activities and duties of the vizier in the state administration, such as the supervision of the foreign delegations that arrived in Egypt to bring tributes to the pharaoh, or tax collection in the country, or oversight and control of various handicrafts activities (sculptures, vases, jewelry, sandals, mortuary regalia, metal processing and brick-making) and food production (wine, bread and honey). Another scene depicts the procession and funerary rituals carried out after the death of this high-ranking official, including the Opening of the Mouth ceremony and the funerary banquet.

158 BOTTOM RIGHT - THE FUNERAL PROCESSION FOR THE BURIAL OF REKHMIRE' OCCUPIES SEVERAL REGISTERS OF THE VIZIER'S TOMB PASSAGEWAY.

159 TOP - IN THE FOREGROUND IS THE NECROPOLIS OF SHEIKH 'ABD EL-QURNA AND IN THE BACKGROUND IS THE DEIR EL-BAHRI CLIFF.

159 BOTTOM RIGHT - A LONG DECORATED CORRIDOR LED TO THE NICHE CONTAINING THE STATUES OF REKHMIRE' AND HIS WIFE.

160 - HENUTTAWY, WIFE OF MENNA, IS DEPICTED IN HER HUSBAND'S TOMB HOLDING A CONE OF OINTMENT TO PERFUME HER HAIR.

161 TOP - THE BACK WALL OF THE TRANSVERSE HALL IN THE TOMB OF MENNA HAS A SCENE DEPICTING THE ADORATION OF OSIRIS.

The tomb of Menna (TT 69), a scribe in charge of overseeing the royal harvests, dates from the time of Tuthmosis IV and Amenhotep III. This has the T-shaped layout typical of early 18th-Dynasty architecture. The multicolored paintings that decorate the walls provide us with a lively representation of the agricultural activities and everyday farm life of the time, with the deceased present as the official supervisor. Other scenes are connected to funerary beliefs and practices, such as the procession of the bark to the necropolis of Abydos, the Opening of the Mouth ceremony, and hunting and fishing in the marshes.

The astronomer of the Temple of Karnak at the time of Tuthmosis IV, Nakht, was buried in Tomb TT 52I, which contains splendid paintings connected with the celebration of the Beautiful Feast of the Valley ceremony and the memory of the deceased. Outstanding among these are the scenes of agricultural and grape harvest work and portraits of musicians, including three girls playing the harp, lute and flute.

161 CENTER LEFT AND **161** BOTTOM – A WALL IN THE TRANSVERSE HALL IN THE TOMB OF MENNA IS DECORATED WITH SCENES OF AGRICULTURAL ACTIVITY.

161 CENTER RIGHT – BIRDS AND BUTTERFLIES FLYING OFF A PAPYRUS PLANT IN THIS DETAIL OF A FISHING SCENE IN THE TOMB OF MENNA.

The tomb of Sennefer (TT 96), the mayor of Thebes during the reign of Amenhotep II, is also called the "tomb of the grapevines" because of the decorative motif of bunches of grapes painted on the ceiling, as well as for the marvelous representation of the deceased together with his wives.

The tomb of Khaemat (TT 57), overseer of the harvests during the reign of Amenhotep III, marks an evolution in the T-shaped layout of the tombs with the addition of an entrance chamber. The relief decoration on the walls consists of detailed representations of farm life, while some niches contain the statues of the deceased, his wife, and the scribe Imhotep.

Another very interesting tomb in the Sheik 'Abd el-Qurna necropolis is the one cut out of the rock for Ra'mose (TT 55), who was vizier under Akhenaten. The unfinished decoration in the first hypostyle hall consists of large, unpainted reliefs that bear witness to the level of artistic refinement achieved in the 'Armana period: the funerary scenes of the presentation of offerings and the funerary banquet are laid out in two registers, while the representation of the deceased's funeral with the transport of the grave goods and the mourners covering their hair with ashes is painted. One of the reliefs, which was later partly erased, shows Ra'mose being rewarded with gold by the pharaoh and his consort, Amenhotep IV and Nefertiti, who appear in a window in the royal palace surmounted by the solar disk of Aten. This is a rare example of Armanian art at Thebes.

162 TOP - RA'MOSE'S SERVANTS TRANSPORT THE DECEASED'S GRAVE GOODS IN A SCENE PAINTED IN THE TRANSVERSE HALL OF THIS 18TH-DYNASTY THEBAN TOMB.

162 BOTTOM - THE TRANSVERSE HALL IN THE TOMB OF RA'MOSE WAS VERY LARGE AND CONTAINED 32 PAPYRUS BUNDLE COLUMNS.

163 - A GROUP OF MOURNERS DRESSED IN WHITE EXPRESSES ITS GRIEF AT THE FUNERAL PROCESSION OF RA'MOSE IN THIS SCENE THAT DECORATES HIS TOMB.

164-165 - THE TOMB OF RA'MOSE HAS SPLENDID RELIEFS PORTRAYING THE PERSONS PRESENT AT HIS FUNERAL BANQUET.

In the necropolis of Sheikh 'Abd el-Qurna there are also tombs dating from the 19th Dynasty. This is the case of the one belonging to Userhat (TT 51), a priest during the time of Ramesses I and Sethos I, which is decorated with scenes of the funerary and divine cult, or in the tomb of Nakhtamon (TT 341), a priest at the Ramesseum in the reign of Ramesses II, with the representation of priests engaged in cult practices.

In the plain facing the locality of Deir el Bahri ('Asasif) lie the tombs of other officials, most of whom lived in the Late Period, while others were active during the New Kingdom. The tomb of Kheruef (TT 192), superintendent of Queen Teye during the reigns of Amenhotep III and IV, is the largest in the Theban necropolis. The structure of this edifice, which is now in ruins, consisted of a long corridor leading to a large court with columned porticoes, a transverse hall supported by columns, and a square pillared chamber. The elegant relief wall decoration that has been preserved shows scenes of the royal festival of Amenhotep III, who, together with his consort Teye, is witnessing the rituals prepared in his honor by Kheruef himself. In the necropolis of el-Khokha, again in the vicinity of Deir el-Bahari, the tomb of Neferrenpet, known as Kenro (TT 178), the scribe of the treasury of the Temple of Amun-Re' under Ramesses II, has funerary scenes articulated on two registers and separated by yellow-ocher bands with inscriptions and decorative friezes. Other New Kingdom tombs lie in the necropolises of Dra Abu el-Naga and el-Tarif, situated north of Deir el-Bahri and already used during the Middle Kingdom and the Second Intermediate Period.

166 - A RELIEF IN THE TOMB OF KHERUEF THAT SHOWS AMENHOTEP III AND QUEEN TEYE PARTICIPATING IN THE JUBILEE CELEBRATIONS. BELOW THEM IS A LIST OF THE POPULATIONS THAT EGYPT HAD DEFEATED.

167 TOP - A GROUP OF FOUR GIRLS ILLUSTRATED IN THE TOMB OF KHERUEF.

167 CENTER - IN THIS SCENE IN THE TOMB OF USERHAT, THE PRIEST IS MAKING OFFERINGS IN THE PRESENCE OF THE GOD OSIRIS.

167 BOTTOM - A WOMAN IS HOLDING A SISTRUM AND RODS IN THIS ILLUSTRATION IN THE ANTECHAMBER OF THE TOMB OF USERHAT.

ARTISTS AND WORKMEN AT DEIR EL-MEDINA

In one of the wadis situated among the Theban hills on the west bank of the Nile, in the vicinity of the Valley of the Queens, lie the ruins of the village of Deir el-Medina. This small town, situated in an isolated position in the desert valley, was in the New Kingdom the center of the community of workmen, artists and artisans who worked on the construction of the royal tombs during the 18th, 19th, and 20th dynasties. This is considered a major archaeological site because it has provided us with numerous, very important documents that have allowed scholars to reconstruct the daily life of a community of private citizens at the time of the New Kingdom. The village, which was probably founded during the reign of Amenhotep I, was laid out around a central street that divided the settlement into two main quarters that were connected by perpendicular streets. Surrounded by a wall, the village had only one entrance gate, to the north, guarded by an edifice used as a watchtower. The 68 houses, which could take in as many as 120 families, were made up of three rooms and a kitchen in the back. The first room had a small altar for worship of the domestic gods; the second, supported by a wooden column, had a seat and some niches in the walls; the third one was probably used as a bedroom and sort of closet. A stairway led to the roof, where there was a terrace used as a family room. In the vicinity of the village were some cult sites, in particular a sanctuary dedicated to the cow goddess Hathor that was enlarged during the Ramessid period and then rebuilt under the Ptolemy rulers. Among the most popular divinities at Deir el-Medina were the goddess Hathor, the god Ptah and the serpent goddess Meresger, as well as the deified figures of Amenhotep I and Queen 'Ahmose-Nefertiry.

Near the village, the inhabitants cut a deep well into the rock, with the hope of reaching the aquifer in order to have an available water supply nearby, without having to go the valley to get it. Here, archaeologists discovered several documents written on *ostraca* or fragments of figured vases, that provide us with a lively description of the daily life in ancient Deir el-Medina.

168 - THIS *OSTRAKON* (H. 4 1/4 IN, 11 CM) WAS FOUND AT DEIR EL-MEDINA AND HOLDS A DEPICTION OF A CAT WITH A STAFF LEADING SIX GEESE (EGYPTIAN MUSEUM, CAIRO).

169 - AERIAL VIEW OF THE SITE OF DEIR EL-MEDINA SHOWING THE LAYOUT OF THIS VILLAGE OF WORKMEN AND ARTISANS, WHOSE HOUSES ARE ATTACHED TO ONE ANOTHER.

171 bottom - The external
coffin of Sennedjem (h. 6 ft,
1.84 m), made during the
Ramessid period, was found in
his tomb at Deir el Medina
(Egyptian Museum, Cairo).

On the slopes of the hills flanking the west side of the village is the necropolis where the citizens of Deir el-Medina were buried, with decorated tombs dating from the 18th Dynasty and the reign of Ramesses II. The tombs were made up of an open court with a small entrance pylon, at whose end was a vaulted funerary chapel surmounted by a small pyramid made of bricks. From the court or the chapel, a vertical shaft led to the underground burial chamber. Some such chambers in this necropolis still have their original polychrome decoration, with panels and paintings containing funerary texts and motifs connected to the Afterlife and modeled after the *Book of the Dead*.

Among the tombs at Deir el-Medina, an outstanding one belongs to the workman Sennedjem (TT 1), which was discovered intact in 1886, decorated with paintings that portray the deceased and his wife in the presence of the funerary divinities. Sennedjem's two children were also buried in his tomb, as can be seen by the sarcophagi and part of the grave goods that are now kept in the Egyptian Museum, Cairo. The tomb of Pashedu (TT 3), a stonecutter during the time of Ramesses II who later became an overseer, has some vividly realistic scenes, such as the one that portrays the deceased kneeling while drinking at the foot of a palm tree. The tomb of Inerkhau (TT 359), the foreman of the village in the 20th Dynasty, is the only tomb in the Deir el-Medina necropolis with scenes representing episodes of the daily life. One interesting scene shows Inerkhau with his wife while he is bringing offerings to the statues of the deceased pharaohs and queens of the New Kingdom. The ceiling of the first hall in this tomb is decorated with unusual motifs: plants, rosettes, spirals and heads of cows. The tomb of the architect Kha and his wife Merit, who lived in the mid-18th Dynasty, was discovered in the Deir el-Medina necropolis. The sepulcher was not decorated, but since it had not been pillaged it still contained the grave goods, which are now at the Egyptian Museum, Turin. Among the precious objects are the sarcophagi containing the mummies, the golden mask placed on the face of Merit, a coffer with toilet articles, fabrics and clothing, a game board, offerings of food, and a measuring instrument covered with gold leaf that a pharaoh gave to the architect.

170-171 - The vault of
the burial chamber
in the tomb of Sennedjem
is decorated with eight
panels containing scenes
from the Book of
the Dead.

171 top - On the back wall
of the burial chamber of
Sennedjem, the deceased
is depicted working in the
fields in the Afterlife. On
the wall at left is a
portrait of Osiris.

172 - ACCESS TO THE BURIAL CHAMBER
OF PASHED IS GAINED BY MEANS OF A
CORRIDOR PAINTED WITH THE FIGURE OF
A JACKAL LYING IN A SACELLUM.

173 - A LARGE *UDJAT* EYE SUPPORTS A
BRAZIER, UNDER WHICH PASHED IS
WORSHIPPING, WITH THE ROCKY THEBAN
MOUNTAIN IN THE BACKGROUND.

Ancient Egyptian culture was permeated with religion and mythological representations. Since prehistoric times there had been a development of religious beliefs that comprised the worship of several gods, the celebration of funerary rituals, and the existence of private cult rituals. The Egyptian pantheon consisted of a great number of divinities, whose characteristics, functions and distinguishing features often overlapped in a rather fluid system of beliefs that was not structured organically. The gods could be represented anthropomorphically, with human bodies and animal heads, or simply as animals. The origin of most of the venerated gods was purely local and dated from the predynastic periods, when Egypt was still split into several independent political states. During the course of Egyptian history, some of these local gods became national divinities and were therefore worshipped throughout the country. There existed various mythical representations of the creation of the world, which inevitably had a creator god who gave birth to various divine couples. The most important cosmogonies were conceived and elaborated in the cities of Heliopolis, Hermopolis and Memphis. In the sanctuaries, worship was not limited to only one divinity but was directed at a divine triad that consisted of a principal god, his consort, and the child born of their union.

The god-falcon Horus, venerated in the ancient city of Hierakonpolis, was in the Predynastic period associated with the figure of the king whose celestial counterpart he represented. Gradually his figure became part of the mythology connected to the god of the dead, Osiris: Horus was born from the union of Isis with the deceased Osiris, who was assassinated by his brother Seth, the god of the desert and storms, who thus usurped the throne of Egypt. The long disputes and struggles between Horus and Seth for supremacy in the country may have reflected the process of formation of the Egyptian state, as well as representing the typically Egyptian concept of opposition between universal order (Ma'at) and chaos. The pharaoh, as the terrestrial representative of Horus, was continuously called upon to guarantee the maintenance of equilibrium and order of all

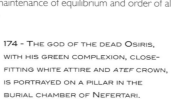

things. With the rise and supremacy of the solar cult of Re', which occurred during the Old Kingdom, the god Horus was assimilated into the celestial god in the form of Re'-Harakhty ("Re'-Horus of the horizon") and depicted with a falcon's head surmounted by a solar disk. The cult of Osiris, the lord of the Afterlife venerated in Abydos, spread from the Old Kingdom on. The myth of his assassination by Seth and his resuscitation by his consort and sister Isis were the basis of Egyptian funerary beliefs and of the concept of rebirth. Represented as a sovereign wrapped in a mummy's cloth, with his dark complexion symbolizing fertility, Osiris judged, by means of a ritual called "psychostasia", the souls of the dead weighing of the deceased's heart on a scale on which had been placed a feather, the symbol of the goddess Ma'at, who represented cosmic order.

The goddess Isis, wife of Osiris and mother of Horus, was one of the main female divinities in the Egyptian pantheon, associated with the concept of maternity. Her figure and representation often mingled with that of the cow goddess Hathor, who was the personification and goddess of the sky, as well as the mistress of song, dance, music and fertility. Depicted as a woman with cow's horns, with the solar disk between them, in the New Kingdom Hathor also became the protector of the necropolises laid out on the west bank of the Nile.

Three especially important divinities in the Egyptian pantheon were linked to the Memphis area and its prominence as the capital of the country in the Old Kingdom. The god Atum, whose cult originated in Heliopolis, was the creator who, according to Heliopolitan theology, generated the divine couples and the world of humans. Often depicted as an elderly man, he was also the sun god in the evening, before it set in the west. The solar cult centered at Heliopolis became consolidated during the Old Kingdom and above all from the 5th Dynasty on; in fact, the sun god Re' was recognized as the principal dynastic god and the pharaohs were considered sons of Re'. The journey of the solar disk in the sky was also associated with the cycle of life and death and with the concept of rebirth connected to funerary beliefs.

174 - THE GOD OF THE DEAD OSIRIS, WITH HIS GREEN COMPLEXION, CLOSE-FITTING WHITE ATTIRE AND *ATEF* CROWN, IS PORTRAYED ON A PILLAR IN THE BURIAL CHAMBER OF NEFERTARI.

175 - RE'-HARAKHTY, HERE DEPICTED IN THE TOMB OF SETHOS I IN THE VALLEY OF THE KINGS, IS A SYNCRETIC DIVINITY WHO IS A COMBINATION OF THE SUN RE' AND THE FALCON HORUS.

The god Ptah was venerated at Memphis as a demiurge of the world and protector of artists. Depicted in the shape of a mummy and wearing a spherical headdress, he was also considered, in the guise of Sokaris, the tutelary god of the Memphite necropolis and was thus connected to the funerary cult. The bull Apis was his sacred animal, venerated especially in the Late Period in the Serapeum at Saqqara. The god's wife was the lioness Sekhmet, and their son was the god Nefertem, depicted with a lotus flower on his head.

In the Middle and New Kingdom a new dynastic divinity came to the fore: the Theban god Amun, originally connected to the atmosphere and to everything invisible. With his association and identification with the sun god Re', in the syncretic guise of Amon-Re', his cult attained primacy, becoming the most important state cult. Amun was considered king of the gods and father of the pharaohs (in the ithyphallic form of Amun-Min-Kamutef), and his principal cult center was Karnak, where the largest temple complex in Egypt was dedicated to him. He was depicted with a human or ram's head, wearing a crown sur-

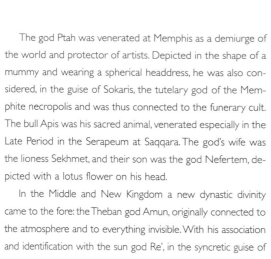

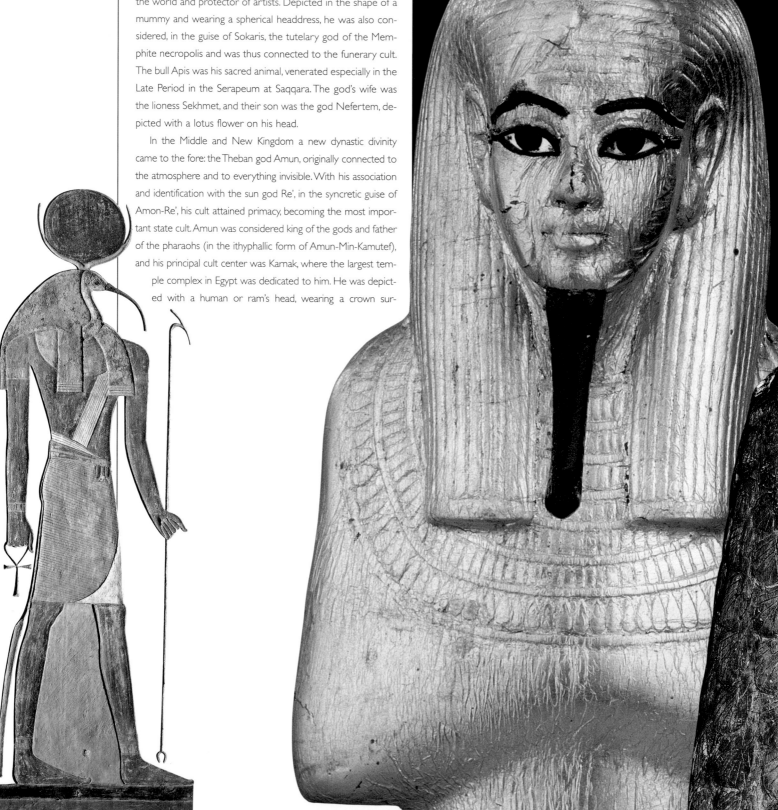

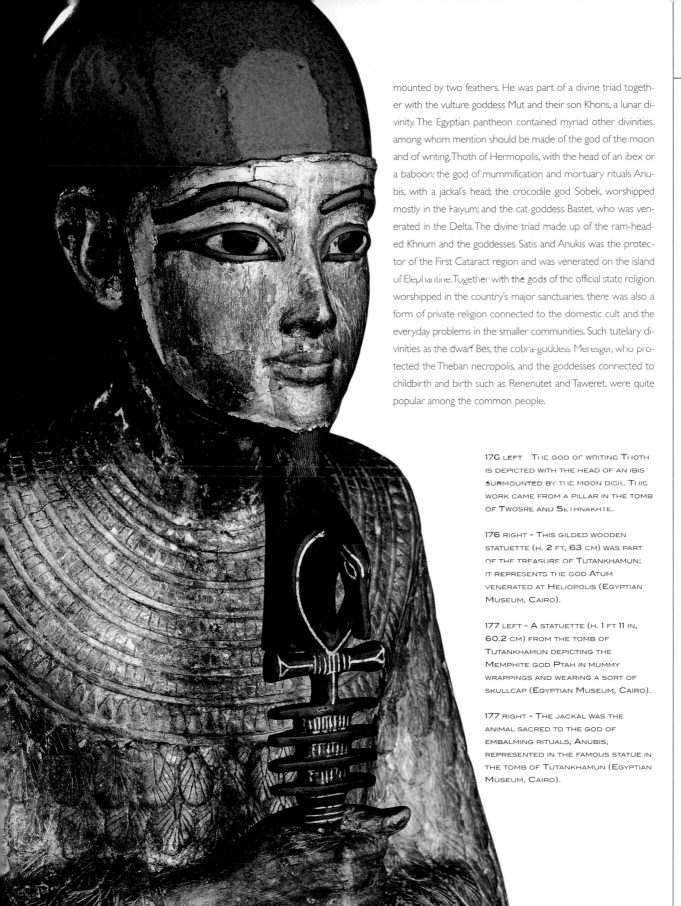

mounted by two feathers. He was part of a divine triad together with the vulture goddess Mut and their son Khons, a lunar divinity. The Egyptian pantheon contained myriad other divinities, among whom mention should be made of the god of the moon and of writing, Thoth of Hermopolis, with the head of an ibex or a baboon; the god of mummification and mortuary rituals Anubis, with a jackal's head; the crocodile god Sobek, worshipped mostly in the Faiyum; and the cat goddess Bastet, who was venerated in the Delta. The divine triad made up of the ram-headed Khnum and the goddesses Satis and Anukis was the protector of the First Cataract region and was venerated on the island of Elephantine. Together with the gods of the official state religion worshipped in the country's major sanctuaries, there was also a form of private religion connected to the domestic cult and the everyday problems in the smaller communities. Such tutelary divinities as the dwarf Bes, the cobra-goddess Meresger, who protected the Theban necropolis, and the goddesses connected to childbirth and birth such as Renenutet and Taweret, were quite popular among the common people.

176 LEFT - THE GOD OF WRITING THOTH IS DEPICTED WITH THE HEAD OF AN IBIS SURMOUNTED BY THE MOON DISK. THIS WORK CAME FROM A PILLAR IN THE TOMB OF TWOSRE AND SETHNAKHTE.

176 RIGHT - THIS GILDED WOODEN STATUETTE (H. 2 FT, 63 CM) WAS PART OF THE TREASURE OF TUTANKHAMUN; IT REPRESENTS THE GOD ATUM VENERATED AT HELIOPOLIS (EGYPTIAN MUSEUM, CAIRO).

177 LEFT - A STATUETTE (H. 1 FT 11 IN, 60.2 CM) FROM THE TOMB OF TUTANKHAMUN DEPICTING THE MEMPHITE GOD PTAH IN MUMMY WRAPPINGS AND WEARING A SORT OF SKULLCAP (EGYPTIAN MUSEUM, CAIRO).

177 RIGHT - THE JACKAL WAS THE ANIMAL SACRED TO THE GOD OF EMBALMING RITUALS, ANUBIS, REPRESENTED IN THE FAMOUS STATUE IN THE TOMB OF TUTANKHAMUN (EGYPTIAN MUSEUM, CAIRO).

THE AFTERLIFE

According to the funerary beliefs elaborated by the ancient Egyptians, life continued after death, but in order for the deceased to enter the Afterlife his/her body had to be preserved intact in the tomb. To this end, tombs that could resist the ravages of time were built, new techniques to preserve the corpse were adopted, and rich grave goods and religious texts accompanied the deceased on their passage to the Afterlife.

When a person died, the first action taken was the mummification of his/her body. This technique, which was probably conceived by observing the natural dehydration of corpses, entailed a long period of immersion in a saline solution (natron), the extraction of the viscera (with the exception of the heart), the filling of the body with wads of linen and with oils and aromatic substances, and lastly the wrapping of the entire body with linen. Several amulets were placed in particular areas of the linen wrappings in order to protect the individual parts of the body from deterioration. Perhaps the most important such amulet was the "scarab of the heart," which was placed on the chest of the mummy and often had a passage from the *Book of the Dead* carved on it. In some cases a sort of death mask was set over the bandages in correspondence with the face of the deceased. The mummy was then put in one or more coffins, the outermost of which was usually made of stone and the innermost of wood. In the most ancient periods these sarcophagi had a parallelepiped shape, while in the Middle Kingdom the anthropoid model became widespread, usually used as the inner coffin. The Old Kingdom sarcophagi were usually decorated with the "palace façade" motif, while in

178-179 - THE MUMMY CASE (L. 6 FT 10 IN, 2.1 M) OF SENBI, A NOMARCH BURIED AT MEIR IN THE 12TH DYNASTY, HAS "PALACE FAÇADE" DECORATION THAT ALTERNATES WITH A SERIES OF DOORS, ONE OF WHICH IS SURMOUNTED BY TWO *UDJAT* EYES (EGYPTIAN MUSEUM, CAIRO).

the Middle Kingdom it became common practice to have them carved with funerary texts known as the *Book of the Sarcophagi*. During the New Kingdom, and above all in the Late Period, there was a great increase in the representations on the sarcophagi of scenes with highly symbolic meaning. On the exterior, the scenes most used depicted the deceased making offerings to the gods, while on the inside the coffin cover represented the sky (in the guise of the goddess Nut) and the bottom the earth (in the guise of the goddess of the west, Imentet), although there were a great many decorative variations. The Late Period witnessed the creation of impressive anthropoid sarcophagi made of basalt, as well as the introduction of the practice of enclosing the entire mummy in a wrapping made of linen, papyrus and painted plaster known as *cartonnage*.

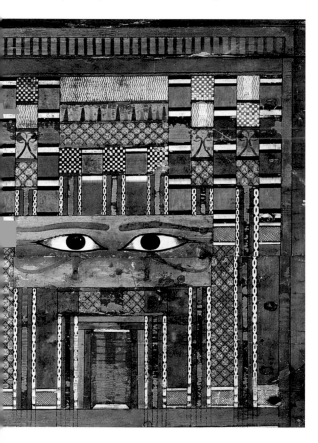

179 - THE SARCOPHAGUS (H. 6 FT 2 IN, 1.9 M) OF A 21 ST-DYNASTY PRIEST NAMED PAKHAR FOUND AT DEIR EL-BAHRI IS DECORATED ON THE EXTERIOR WITH SCENES OF DIVINITIES AND ON THE INSIDE WITH A LARGE FIGURE OF A WINGED GODDESS (EGYPTIAN MUSEUM, CAIRO).

Next to the sarcophagus in the tomb lay the grave goods, which were intended to guarantee the deceased's existence in the Afterlife. The goods varied according to the period and the social status of the deceased. Among the most important were the so-called canopic jars, receptacles used to preserve the viscera extracted from the corpse and mummified separately. In the Old Kingdom these vessels were quadripartite cases, while in the Middle Kingdom they took on the shape of vases whose covers or stoppers had human features. In the New Kingdom the covers were in the form of the heads of the four sons of Horus (Imset, Ha'py, Duamutef and Qebehsenuf), whose function was to protect the viscera.

Other very important and widespread objects from the end of the Middle Kingdom on were the funerary statuettes known as *Shabti* ("The Answerers"). These objects, shaped like mummies, and collected in special containers, were designed to act as servants of the deceased by carrying out the more difficult tasks assigned to him/her in the Afterlife. The grave goods then included jewels, personal objects, clothing, furniture, other furnishings, food, and cosmetics – all depending, naturally, on the economic status of the deceased. During the New Kingdom, buried with the body of the deceased was a papyrus containing the funerary text of the *Book of the Dead*, a collection of religious formulas accompanied by painted illustrations, whose most famous scene depicted the weighing of the deceased's heart. The ceremony that accompanied the deceased to the tomb had the characteristics of a funeral procession and symbolically referred to the pilgrimage to the city of Abydos, the burial place of the god Osiris. Once in the tomb, the mummy went through the Opening of the Mouth ceremony, which was officiated by a priest wearing a leopard skin (the *sem* or mortuary priest), which restored life to the deceased. Once the tomb was sealed, the funerary ritual that guaranteed passage to the Afterlife was entrusted to the deceased's relatives and to priests, who continuously had to place funerary offerings in the tomb chapels.

181 RIGHT - THE ALABASTER CONTAINER
(H. 2 FT 9 IN, 85.5 CM) WITH
TUTANKHAMUN'S CANOPIC JARS, WHOSE
LIDS REPRODUCE THE PHARAOH'S
LIKENESS, LIES ON A SLEDGE (EGYPTIAN
MUSEUM, CAIRO).

180 - THE CANOPIC JARS OF PSUSENNES I
(H. 15–17 IN, 38-43 CM), WHICH WERE
FOUND AT TANIS, HAVE LIDS REPRESENTING
THE HEADS OF THE FOUR SONS OF HORUS
(EGYPTIAN MUSEUM, CAIRO).

181 LEFT - THIS SANCTUARY, MADE OF GILDED
WOOD AND WITH A BALDACHIN (H. 6FT 2 IN,
1.9 M), CONTAINED THE CANOPIC JARS OF
TUTANKHAMUN (EGYPTIAN MUSEUM, CAIRO).

5

THE LATE PERIOD
AND THE AGE OF FOREIGN DOMINION

THE THIRD INTERMEDIATE PERIOD

With the ascension to the throne of Smendes, the first pharaoh of the 21st Dynasty (1075–945 BC), began another period of political fragmentation that scholars usually refer to as the Third Intermediate Period. Smendes moved the capital from Pi-Ri'amese to Tanis, in the eastern Delta area, and reused many of the monuments that Ramesses II had erected. The new pharaoh's power was formally recognized by the High Priest of Amun at Thebes, Pinudjem, who really controlled Upper Egypt and the Thebes region. The power of the Amun priests was guaranteed by the figure of the so-called Divine Adoratrice, a priestess in charge of the cult of the god Amun who was obliged to remain unmarried and who, being a member of the royal family, was entitled to pass on her office through the system of "adoption." Smendes's successor, Psusennes I, seems to have initiated work on the construction of the sanctuary of Amun at Tanis, whose layout was meant to mirror that of the Great Temple of Karnak. Archaeological excavations in the sacred precinct of this temple, headed by Pierre Montet in the 1930s, brought to light the tombs of some 21st- and 22nd-Dynasty kings, together with their rich royal regalia and grave goods. Among the most precious objects were the silver coffins of Psusennes I and Shoshenq II and their respective gold funerary masks, the death masks of Amenemope and the general Undjebauendjed, and a great number of vases, paterae, jars, bowls, and jewelry made of precious metal and stones. During the 21st Dynasty the High Priest of Amun, Pinudjem II, a contemporary of the pharaoh Siamun,

transferred the principal New Kingdom royal mummies from their original tombs, which during the turbulent final period of the New Kingdom had been violated, to two tombs used as hiding places (the one belonging to Amenhotep II in the Valley of the Kings, and the tomb of Queen Inhapi [TT 320] at Deir el-Bahri), where the mummies were found in the late 1800s. In the 22nd Dynasty (945–718 BC) power passed into the hands of a royal family of Libyan origin. The best-known ruler is the first pharaoh Shoshenq I who carried out works in the first court of the Karnak temple, where he ordered some scenes to be carved commemorating his victories over the kingdoms of Judaea and Israel. Very little is known concerning the history of the Shoshenq I's successors: a bust of Osorkon I, found at Byblos, suggests that there may have been active diplomatic relations with the cities along the Palestinian coast. At Bubastis in the Delta, Osorkon II built a portico, some fragments and reliefs of which have survived. Two masterpieces of ancient Egyptian jewelry-making date to the 22nd Dynasty: a gold and lapis lazuli pendant with a portrait of the Osirian triad and the bronze statuette with inlaid gold, silver and electrum of the Divine Adoratrice Karomama, the daughter of Osorkon II. The end of the 22nd Dynasty was marked by dynastic struggles that involved the rulers of the Delta and the Theban high priests. The political chaos and anarchy that ensued was further complicated when a new noble family from Leontopolis arrogated to itself the right to govern and thus founded a parallel dynasty, the 23rd (820–718 BC).

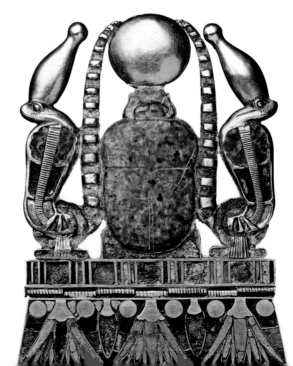

183 - THIS 2ND-CENTURY AD FUNERARY PORTRAIT OF TWO BROTHERS (H. 2 FT, 61 CM) COMES FROM ANTINOOPOLIS (EGYPTIAN MUSEUM, CAIRO).

184 - THIS GOLD, LAPIS LAZULI AND FAÏENCE PECTORAL (H. 2 3/4 IN, 7 CM) WAS FOUND IN THE TOMB OF SHOSHENQ II AT TANIS (EGYPTIAN MUSEUM, CAIRO).

185 - THE GOLD DEATH MASK OF PSUSENNES I (H. 19 IN, 48 CM), FOUND IN THE ROYAL NECROPOLIS OF TANIS, IS ONE OF THE GREATEST TREASURES OF ANCIENT EGYPTIAN ART. IN PSUSENNES I'S TOMB PIERRE MONTET BROUGHT TO LIGHT THE RICH GRAVE GOODS OF OTHER PROTAGONISTS OF THE 21ST DYNASTY (EGYPTIAN MUSEUM, CAIRO).

While Osorkon IV (22nd Dynasty) and Iuput II (23rd Dynasty) ruled in the Delta, the prince of Sais, Tefnakhte, founder of the 24th Dynasty (730–712 BC), headed a coalition with the aim of repulsing the advance of an army that was moving up the course of the Nile from distant Nubia with the intention of reunifying Egypt under a single crown. The leader of this military expedition was Piye (745–713 BC), the ruler of a Nubian (or Kushite) dynasty centered in the city of Napata, at the foot of Mt. Gebel Barkal, in the Fourth Cataract region. During his march toward the Delta, Piye had already succeeded in extending his dominion over the Theban region and had installed his sister Amenirdis I as the Divine Adoratrice of Amun. Piye got the better of Tefnakhte and obtained the submission of the sovereigns of the Delta, who acknowledged him as the legiti-

mate ruler, but strangely enough he immediately returned with his army to Nubia. He had himself buried under a small pyramid in the necropolis of el-Kurru. Shabaka, Piye's brother, again unified Egypt under a single crown, bringing the 24th Dynasty to an end. Having established peace in the country, the pharaohs of the 25th Dynasty (713–653 BC) undertook a policy of restoring ancient Egyptian traditions, as is demonstrated by the religious text *Memphite Theology*, which harked back to the most ancient Old Kingdom models. Taharqa was the most active Kushite ruler: in Nubia (at Semna, Buhen, Kawa, Sanam he built a set of temples consecrated to the god Amun, while at Napata he enlarged the Temple of Amun (B 500) and had another one dedicated to the goddess Mut cut out of the living rock; and in Egypt he made some changes to the temple of Karnak and restored other temples. His power at Thebes seems to have been exercised with the aid of the fourth prophet of Amun, Mentuemhet, whom we know well because of the numerous statues portraying him, as well as his monumental tomb in the necropolis of 'Asasif. The final years of Taharqa's rule were characterized by military defeats: first the Assyrian king Esarhaddon, and then his successor Assurbanipal invaded Egypt, sacking the cities. The last Kushite pharaoh, Tantamani, was forced to retreat to Nubia, thus marking the end of Nubian dominion over Egypt. The Assyrians did not directly control Egypt, but chose to entrust the task of governing to local princes they deemed trustworthy, the most outstanding of whom was Psammetichus I of Sais, the founder of the 26th Dynasty (664–525 BC), who succeeded in having himself recognized as the sole pharaoh. In the 26th Dynasty, Egypt opened its doors to the Mediterranean world, through the foundation of a Greek trading emporium at Naukratis in the Delta, the enlistment of Greek and Carian mercenaries in the Egyptian army, and the establishment of diplomatic alliances with the world of the Greek *poleis*. In 525 BC the Persian army led by Cambyses invaded Egypt, defeating Psammetichus III's army and imposing his supremacy over Egypt, which was transformed into a satrap of the great Achaemenid Empire.

186 - THE STATUE OF THE DIVINE ADORATRICE AMENIRDIS I (H. 5 FT 6 IN, 1.7 M), WHO IS WEARING A WIG COVERED BY THE WINGS OF A FALCON AND WITH HIS FOREHEAD WRAPPED IN A DOUBLE URAEUS (EGYPTIAN MUSEUM, CAIRO).

187 - THIS HEAD FROM SAIS (H. 9 1/2 IN, 24 CM) IS ATTRIBUTED TO THE 26TH-DYNASTY KING AMASIS (EGYPTIAN MUSEUM, BERLIN).

Among the architectural works realized in the 25th and 26th Dynasties are the preserved funerary chapels of the Divine Adoratrices of Amun built in front of the entrance pylon of the mortuary temple of Ramesses III at Medinet Habu, and the monumental tombs in the 'Asasif necropolis constructed for leading Theban dignitaries. One building in particular took on importance during the course of the 26th Dynasty: the Serapeum of Memphis. This edifice, situated west of Djoser's funerary complex at Saqqara, consists of a network of underground galleries used as the burial site of the Apis bulls, animals sacred to the Memphite god Ptah.

Persian dominion over Egypt, indicated as the 27th Dynasty (525–404 BC), has left few archaeological traces, the most important of which is a temple dedicated to the Theban triad, built by Darius I in the Kharga Oasis. The person who put an end to Persian dominion after the death of Darius II in 404 BC, was a Saite prince, Amyrtaios, the only king of the 28th Dynasty (404–399 BC); the following dynasty (399–380 BC), which originated in Mendes in the Delta, forged alliances with the Greek cities as an anti-Persian move. In 380 BC a general from Sebennytos in the Delta took power and had himself proclaimed pharaoh with the throne name of Nectanebo I. Thus began the 30th Dynasty (380–342 BC), the last one of local origin to rule Egypt. The pharaohs of this dynasty were the protagonists of a resumption of building activity, as can be seen by the works of Nectanebo I at Karnak, Philae and Dendara. In 343 BC the Persian army, led by their king Artaxerxes III, invaded Egypt and defeated Nectanebo II, marking the demise of Egyptian independence. The long history of the pharaonic dynasties was thus approaching its end, but this did not come about because of any action by the Persians. After the brief reign of a king named Khababash, in 332 BC the Macedonian ruler Alexander the Great conquered the country without a struggle and had himself proclaimed pharaoh by the oracle of Ammon in the Siwa oasis.

189 RIGHT - THE CULT OF THE BULL-HEADED GOD APIS AT THE SERAPEUM OF SAQQARA WAS VERY POPULAR DURING THE PTOLEMAIC PERIOD, AS CAN BE SEEN IN THIS STELE (H. 1 FT 2 IN, 35 CM) WITH A GREEK INSCRIPTION (EGYPTIAN MUSEUM, CAIRO).

188 - THE PERSIAN DYNASTY TEMPLE AT QASR EL-GHUEIDA, IN THE KHARGA OASIS, WAS DEDICATED TO THE THEBAN TRIAD AND DECORATED DURING THE PTOLEMAIC PERIOD.

189 TOP - BRONZE STATUETTE (H. 10 1/4 IN, 26 CM), FROM SAQQARA OF A LATE PERIOD KING WHO IS KNEELING WHILE MAKING AN OFFERING OF AN UDJAT EYE (EGYPTIAN MUSEUM, CAIRO).

THE PTOLEMAIC AND ROMAN PERIOD

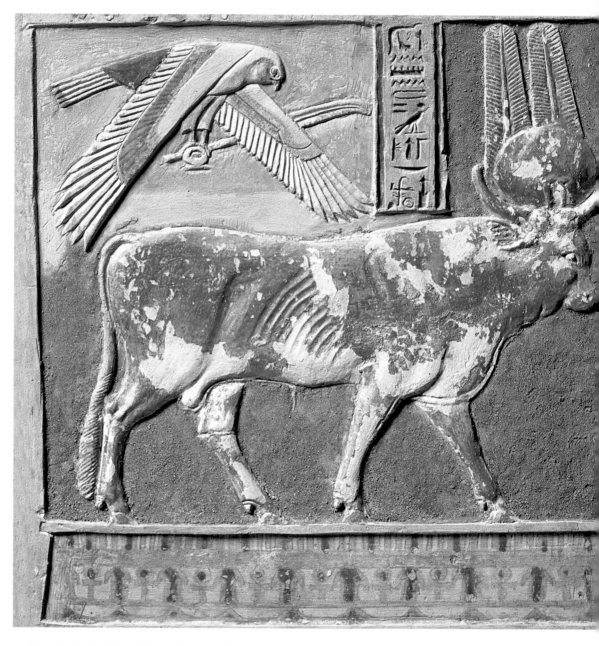

Upon the death of Alexander the Great, who founded the important coastal city of Alexandria in the Delta, control over the country was taken by a Macedonian general, Ptolemy, whose family then ruled for the following 270 years. The Ptolemies had themselves represented as Egyptian pharaohs, but refused to renounce their Greek origin and culture. The cult of the ancient Egyptian gods was maintained, yet divinities of the Greek pantheon were introduced into the country, which led to the birth of syncretic forms, the most famous of

which was the god Serapis, a divinity that combined the characteristics of Osiris, the Apis bull, Zeus, Hades and Asclepius.

Alexandria soon became a cosmopolitan city open to the various influences from the Mediterranean region and frequented by poets, artists and scientists. Its museum and library became a reference point and cultural model for the other Mediterranean populations. Most of the Ptolemaic monuments in Alexandria no longer exist, but certain accounts of the time are beginning to emerge from the waters opposite

the city port thanks to a program of underwater archaeological excavation. Greek became the court language, while the public documents were written in both Greek and Demotic, the later form of the ancient Egyptian written in simplified script. An example of the coexistence of the two languages is the famous Rosetta Stone, a royal decree written in three languages (Egyptian hieroglyphics, Egyptian Demotic and Greek) at the time of Ptolemy V (196 BC), which in 1822 allowed Jean-François Champollion to decipher hieroglyphic script for the first time. In the mid-2nd century BC Ptolemaic Egypt entered a period marked by economic crises, dynastic strife and domestic rebellions. In 31 BC the defeat of Mark Antony in the Battle of Actium and the successive death of Cleopatra VII left Egypt in the hands of Octavius (later the Emperor Augustus), who made the country a province of the Roman Empire. Egyptian monuments began to be transported to Rome, mainly the obelisks erected by the pharaohs, which still decorate many squares of that city. But Egyptian customs and styles also became fashionable in ancient Rome, so much so that one Roman citizen, a certain Caius Cestius Aepulon, asked to be buried in a pyramid shaped tomb. The Emperor Hadrian was a great admirer of Egyptian civilization and culture, and in fact decorated his famous villa at Tivoli with Egyptian-style edifices and statues. Some ancient Egyptian cults, such as those of Isis or Serapis, spread throughout the imperial provinces, and many sanctuaries and temples dedicated to these gods were founded in various parts of the Mediterranean. The rise of Christianity in the Roman Empire in the 4th century AD marked the beginning of the end for Egyptian tradition: in 391 AD the Emperor Theodosius ordered that all pagan places of worship be closed. Three years later, the last hieroglyphic inscription known to us was carved on a wall of the Temple of Philae.

190-191 - ON THIS STELE PTOLEMY V MAKES AN OFFERING TO THE BULL BUCHIS, THE ANIMAL ASSOCIATED WITH THE FALCON GOD MONTU OF ARMANT (H. 2 FT 4 IN, 72 CM; EGYPTIAN MUSEUM, CAIRO).

191 - A ROMAN PERIOD ALABASTER BUST (H. 7 IN, 17.5 CM) REPRESENTING ZEUS-SERAPIS, A SYNCRETIC DEITY WHO WAS PARTICULARLY POPULAR DURING THE GRECO-ROMAN AGE (EGYPTIAN MUSEUM, CAIRO).

The Ptolemaic sovereigns and Roman emperors in Egypt erected temples modeled after the local architectural styles and had themselves portrayed on the walls in the same manner as the ancient pharaohs. The temple of Dendara, along a curve of the Nile in the province of Qena, was dedicated to the cow goddess Hathor. The sacred precinct, access to which was afforded by a monumental gate built by the Roman Emperors Domitian and Trajan, contained the main temple and some subsidiary buildings. Among these were two *mammisi* (edifices used to celebrate the birth of the son of the divine

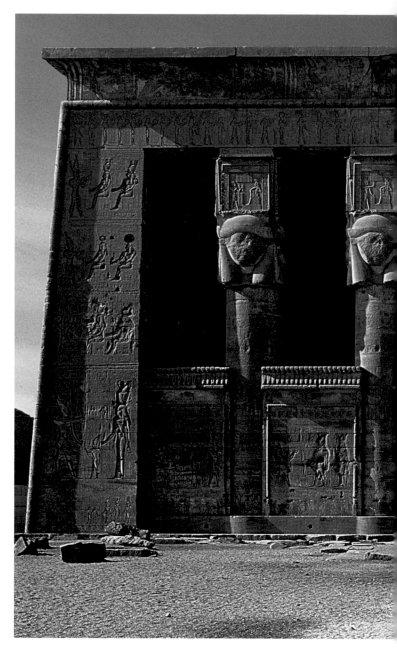

triad worshipped in this locality), one dating to the Roman period and other to the 30th Dynasty, and a temple dedicated to the birth of Isis, built during the reign of the Emperor Augustus. On the façade of the main temple are six columns with a capital in the shape of a Hathoric sistrum that are separated from one another by a wall-balustrade. In the interior, two hypostyle halls precede the sanctuary of the sacred bark, which has several chapels on three sides. The first hypostyle hall, whose ceiling is decorated with astronomical scenes, contains 18 columns with a Hathoric capital; the second one, which is smaller, is supported by six Hathoric columns. Surrounding the central sanctuary are 11 chapels consecrated to the same number of divinities. Below these chapels are rock-cut chambers with relief sculpture decoration that were probably used as storerooms and areas for rituals. In the west section of the temple, facing a small outdoor court, is a small chapel ("pure chapel"), which is framed by two columns with

a Hathoric sistrum, on whose ceiling is a portrait of the goddess of the sky Nut generating the Sun, which with its rays illuminates and gives life to the goddess Hathor. On the roof of the Dendara temple, which was a true terrace accessible by means of two stairways, there were some chapels and a kiosk for the celebration of the union of the goddess and the solar disk. One of these chapels contained the famous relief decoration of the Zodiac that is now kept in the Louvre, Paris.

192 top - The Zodiac of
Dendera (l. 8 ft, 2.5 m)
represents the heaven,
with the constellations
and signs of the zodiac
(Louvre, Paris).

192 bottom - The columns
in the first hypostyle hall
at Dendera have Hathoric
capitals.

192-193 - The façade of
the temple of Dendera
has six columns with
Hathoric capitals.

193 bottom - The temple
of Dendera is preceded
by the ruins of two
mammisi, a Christian
basilica, and a
"sanatorium."

Situated 34 miles (55 km) south of Luxor, the temple of Esna was dedicated to the ram-headed god Khnum, together with other divinities such as Neith, Heka and Satis. The only remaining part of the original sanctuary is the hypostyle hall, which, with its façade bearing six columns with floral capitals, was the temple entrance. The large hypostyle hall is supported by 24 columns with floral capitals that differ from one another. The walls of the halls, decorated by various Roman emperors, have important religious texts, and on the ceiling are Zodiacal scenes.

built during the reign of Nectanebo II. Around the central body of the temple is a wall whose inner sides are decorated with reliefs depicting the foundation of the sanctuary and scenes that accompany a "dramatic" text concerning the triumph of the god Horus over the god Seth.

The temple of Kom Ombo, 27 miles (45 km) north of Aswan, has an unusual layout due to the fact that the sanctuary was dedicated to two divine triads. The eastern half of the temple was reserved for the triad consisting of the crocodile

The temple of Edfu, located 34 miles (56 km) south of Esna, is the best preserved temple in Egypt. Built during the Ptolemaic period, its plan could be considered the prototype of later Greco-Roman temple architecture. The temple, dedicated to the falcon god Horus, is preceded by a pylon, in front of which are two statues of falcons. Behind the pylon is a court with colonnades (with paired capitals all different from one another) decorated with scenes of ceremonies and religious festivals. The façade of the temple has the usual arrangement of six columns separated by wall-balustrades. In front of the entrance there is still a black granite statue of a falcon with a double crown. In the interior, two hypostyle halls supported by 12 columns precede the hall for offerings and a stone *naos*

god Sobek, his wife Hathor and their son Khons, and the western half was for the triad of Haroeris (Horus the Elder), Tasenetnofret and Panebtawy. Thus, the plan of the temple is divided into two sections that mirror each other. Access to the entrance court, surrounded by a colonnade, was through a double gate whose alignment corresponded to the double entrance of the façade. The interior of the temple maintained a bipartite structure: two hypostyle halls, two offerings halls, and two sanctuaries for the sacred bark. A double wall ran around the central body of the temple, forming two passageways decorated with reliefs, among which is the unusual representation of surgical instruments. Outside the temple are the remains of a small chapel dedicated to Hathor and a *mammisi*.

194 - THIS LARGE STATUE OF A FALCON
WITH A DOUBLE CROWN STANDS IN
FRONT OF THE FAÇADE OF THE EDFU
TEMPLE, FLANKING THE ENTRANCE TO
THE FIRST HYPOSTYLE HALL.

195 LEFT - THE FAÇADE OF THE TEMPLE
OF ESNA HAS THE CLASSICAL
STRUCTURE OF GRECO-ROMAN
PERIOD TEMPLES.

195 RIGHT - THE TEMPLE OF KOM
OMBO, SEEN FROM TOP, REVEALS
ITS SINGULAR LAYOUT BASED ON
PARALLEL AXES.

196-197 - THE TEMPLE OF EDFU,
SACRED TO HORUS, IS THE BEST
PRESERVED GRECO-ROMAN EDIFICE IN
EGYPT, AND ITS ENTRANCE PYLON IS
STILL 118 FT (36 M) HIGH.

The temple erected on the island of Philae, which was recently moved to the nearby islet of Agilkia after construction of the High Dam of Aswan, was a major cult center of the goddess Isis, the wife of Osiris. At the southern tip of the island is the most ancient monument, a small kiosk built by Nectanebo I. From here, two long colonnades lead to the main temple. Behind the west colonnade are some small buildings – the temples dedicated to the Nubian gods Arensnuphis and Mandulis, and a sanctuary in honor of Imhotep, the architect of Djoser who was deified in the Late Period. The first pylon of the main temple, on which stands the figure of Ptolemy XII slaying his enemies and

making offerings to Isis, leads to a court with an irregular layout, whose two sides are closed off by a *mammisi* and by a colonnade behind which are some small chambers. The second pylon gives access to a small hypostyle hall and to the inner halls of the sanctuary. On the roof are some chapels dedicated to the god Osiris. To the east of the main sanctuary is a small temple consecrated to Hathor that was built during the reigns of Ptolemy VI and Ptolemy VIII, and near it is a kiosk built by the Emperor Trajan. In the Nubian locality of Kalabsha, which lies about 30 miles (50 km) south of Aswan, the Roman Emperor Augustus finished a temple dedicated to the local sun god Mandulis, with whom he associated the cult of the Egyptian gods Isis and Osiris.

Recently moved to a locality near Aswan in order to protect it from the waters of Lake Nasser, the temple was preceded by a quay. The entrance pylon, which was not aligned with the axis of the temple, gave access to a trapezoid-shaped forecourt with a peristyle on three sides that was decorated by Amenhotep II, Ptolemy IX and some Meroïtic kings. The temple façade has columns with composite floral capitals separated by a wall-balustrade. The interior consists of a hypostyle hall with eight columns that precedes the offerings hall, the sanctuary with the *naos,* and some chapels. The temple is surrounded by two enclosure walls, inside which are a small chapel dedicated to the Nubian god Dedwen and a *mammisi.*

198 - THE SO-CALLED KIOSK OF TRAJAN AT PHILAE, BUILT DURING THE ROMAN PERIOD, HAS DECORATION THAT SHOWS THE EMPEROR MAKING OFFERINGS TO THE GODS OSIRIS, ISIS AND HORUS.

198-199 - THE TEMPLE OF PHILAE, WHICH ONCE STOOD ON THE ISLAND OF THE SAME NAME, WAS MOVED TO THE NEARBY ISLAND OF AGILKIA IN ORDER TO PREVENT IF FROM BEING SUBMERGED BY THE WATERS OF LAKE NASSER.

199 BOTTOM - THE UNFINISHED EAST COLONNADE LEADING TO THE ENTRANCE PYLON OF THE TEMPLE OF PHILAE HAS FLORAL CAPITALS THAT ARE ALL DIFFERENT FROM ONE ANOTHER.

199 RIGHT - ON THE ENTRANCE PYLON OF THE TEMPLE OF PHILAE IS THE FIGURE OF THE GOD HORUS, OPPOSITE WHOM (BUT NOT SEEN IN THIS PHOTO) IS PTOLEMY XII KILLING HIS ENEMIES.

200 CENTER - A GRECO-ROMAN SARCOPHAGUS LID (H. 3 FT, 94 CM) DECORATED WITH THE TERRA-COTTA FIGURE OF A SIREN (EGYPTIAN MUSEUM, CAIRO).

200 BOTTOM - THE NECROPOLIS OF MUSTAFA KAMAL AT ALEXANDRIA HAS UNDERGROUND BURIAL CHAMBERS WITH A CENTRAL COURT WITH DORIC COLUMNS.

200-201 - THE DIRECTOR OF THE EGYPTIAN ANTIQUITIES SERVICE, ZAHI HAWASS, CAREFULLY EXAMINING THE MUMMIES FOUND IN THE BAHARIYA OASIS.

201 - A ROMAN PERIOD PAINTING (H. 3 FT 3 IN, 98 CM) FROM THE NECROPOLIS OF TUNA EL-GEBEL DEPICTING EPISODES FROM THE MYTH OF OEDIPUS (EGYPTIAN MUSEUM, CAIRO).

The necropolises laid out during the Greco-Roman period are among the most obvious examples of the syncretism that was created between Egyptian and Hellenistic culture after Alexander the Great's conquest of Egypt. Petosiris, the high priest of Thoth at the beginning of the Ptolemaic period, had his funerary chapel built in the town of Tuna el-Gebel. This structure looks like a small Egyptian temple. The façade is decorated with scenes rendered in traditional Egyptian style that show Petosiris making offerings to the local god Thoth. In the interior is a *pronaos* decorated with scenes of daily life much like those in the Old Kingdom mastabas, but here the style and rendering

used as a funerary chapel. From here a deep cylindrical shaft with a spiral stairway led to the various levels of the underground areas. The first of these consisted of a vestibule formed by a corridor with a double exedra, a rotunda with a domed ceiling and a central well surrounded by six pillars, and a side triclinium with a couch hewn out of the rock that was used for the funerary banquet. From the rotunda a stairway led to the second level of the complex, where the true tomb was situated. This latter had a layout much like a Greek temple, with a two-column *pronaos* and a *cella*, which in this case served as the burial chamber. The *pronaos* was made up of Egyptian architectural elements: two columns with a composite floral capital and an architrave with a winged solar disk in relief. The reliefs that decorated the burial chamber and the three sarcophagi it houses combine Egyptian and Hellenstic stylistic features, such as the figure of the god Anubis in the guise of a Roman centurion. The central burial chamber was surrounded on three sides by a corridor in which about 300 loculi were cut out of the rock to be used for the burial of persons who were either embalmed, in keeping with Egyptian custom, or cremated, as was common among the ancient Romans. Besides the tombs in Alexandria, there are various Greco-Roman necropolises scattered in the Western Desert oases. In 1999 a vast necropolis from the Roman period was brought to light in the Bahariya oasis, where the locals had themselves buried in underground family tombs. Excavations carried out by the Egyptian Antiquities Service led to the discovery of numerous mummies placed in gilded or painted coffins and sometimes covered with death masks. These finds have provided us with precious information about the Roman period community that lived in this oasis and the funerary techniques and practices of the time. A special category of funerary finds from the Roman period are the so-called Faiyum portraits, painted wooden panels depicting the head of the deceased that were placed on the mummies. Found mostly in the Faiyum and in some localities of Middle Egypt, these portraits represent the deceased with idealized features, but they also dwell on a great many details of contemporaneous customs and fashions, giving us an idea of these aspects of life in Egypt at the time of the Roman Empire.

of the human figures and their clothing reveals the influence of Greek iconography. The tomb proper has yielded the wooden coffins of Petosiris, which have some passages from the *Book of the Dead* inlaid with polychrome glazing. The Hellenistic-Roman population in Alexandria was buried in some city necropolises that reveal the combination of Egyptian elements and Hellenistic funerary practices. The necropolis of Kom el-Shuqafa, which dates to the Roman period and is situated near the ancient port quarter of Rakhotis, is made up of a complex network of catacombs that were deeply cut out of the ground. On the ground, the necropolis was surmounted by a building that was probably

202 AND 203 LEFT - THESE ENCAUSTIC
OR TEMPERA PORTRAITS ON WOODEN
PANELS (H. 12—16 IN, 41—31 CM) ARE
SPLENDID EXAMPLES OF ROMAN PERIOD
FUNERARY ART (EGYPTIAN MUSEUM,
CAIRO).

203 RIGHT - THE MUMMY (H. 4 FT 11 IN,
1.5 M) OF THIS WOMAN BURIED AT
SAQQARA IN THE 4TH CENTURY AD LIES
IN A CARTONNAGE SARCOPHAGUS WITH
POLYCHROME TEMPERA DECORATION
(EGYPTIAN MUSEUM, CAIRO).

GLOSSARY

Atef crown: A headdress traditionally connected to the god Osiris. It consisted of a white crown flanked by two ostrich feathers and surmounted by a small sun disk.

Benben: A conically shaped stone venerated at Heliopolis, identified with the primordial hill from which the world was born and associated with the god Atum.

Cache: Term used to indicate a hiding place where statues were deposited, such as those found under the temples of Karnak and Luxor, or the tombs where the principal New Kingdom royal mummies were hidden.

Faïence: A glassy, bluish-green material made principally of quartz, silicon and mineral oxides that was fired in order to manufacture amulets, necklaces, and inlay work in particular.

Mammisi: A religious edifice connected to a large sanctuary in which the birth of the son of a divine couple was celebrated.

Mastaba: An Arabic word that means "bench" and is used to indicate the tombs in the shape of a parallelepiped typical of the most ancient periods of Egyptian history.

Naos: A small chapel or shrine, usually in a temple sanctuary, that housed the statue of a god.

Nemes: A cloth headdress worn by the Egyptian kings the two sides of which covered the shoulders and chest.

Nome: Term derived from the Greek *nomos* indicating the provinces on which the administrative stystem of ancient Egypt was organized.

Ostrakon: A fragment of pottery or stone used for writing.

Pyramidion: A stone block in the shape of a pyramid that crowned an obelisk or completed the tip of a real pyramid.

Saff Tomb: The typical type of 11th-Dynasty tomb in the Thebes area, characterized by one or two rows of rock-cut pillars that made up the facade.

Sed Festival: A jubilee celebration organized on occasion of a pharaoh's 30th year of reign in order to renew his power; the festival could then be repeated at shorter intervals.

Serdab: Word of Arabic origin indicating the niche or chapel in a tomb in which the statue of the deceased was placed.

Serekh: Rectangle that reproduces the stylized form of a palace, inside which was written the "name of Horus" of a pharaoh. It was usually surmounted by the image of a falcon.

Uraeus: The figure of the cobra connected to the Egyptian concept of royalty worn on the headdresses and crowns of the pharaohs.

INDEX

ALDRED C., *Egyptian art in the days of the pharaohs*. Oxford University Press, New York - Toronto 1980

BAINES J. & MÁLEK J., *Atlas of Ancient Egypt*. Phaidon, Oxford 1985

BRESCIANI E., *Sulle rive del Nilo. L'Egitto al tempo dei faraoni*. Laterza, Rome-Bari 2000

GARDINER A., *Egypt of the Pharaohs. An Introduction*. Oxford University Press, Oxford 1966

GRIMAL N., *Histoire de l'Égypte ancienne*. Fayard, Paris 1988

HAWASS Z., *The treasures of the pyramids*. White Star, Vercelli 2003

HAWASS Z., *The realm of the pharaohs*. White Star, Vercelli 2006

HORNUNG E., *Conceptions of God in Ancient Egypt*. Cornell University Press, Ithaca 1982

KEMP B.J., *Ancient Egypt: Anatomy of a Civilization*. Routledge, London 1989

LICHTEIM M., *Ancient Egyptian Literature*. 3 vols. University of California Press, Berkeley 1973-1980

MALEK J., *Egyptian Art. Phaidon*, London 1999

MIDANT-REYNES, *Préhistoire de l'Égypte*. Armand Colin, Paris 1992

TIRADRITTI F., *Tesori egizi nella collezione del Museo Egizio del Cairo*. White Star, Vercelli 2000

TRIGGER B.G. ET AL., *Ancient Egypt: A Social History*. Cambridge University, Cambridge 1983

VALBELLE D., *Histoire de l'État pharaonique*. Puf, Paris 1998

VERNUS P. - YOYOTTE J., *Dictionnaire des Pharaons*. Noêsis, Paris 1996

WEEKS K.R. (ed.), *Valley of the King. The tombs and the funerary temples of Thebes west*. White Star, Vercelli 2002

Giorgio Ferrero was born in Milan in 1978. He graduated in Egyptology with a thesis on Ancient Nubia and has collaborated with the Egyptology Department of the Università degli Studi of Milan and with the Archeological and Numismatic Civic Collections of Milan. He has published *Wonders of Egypt* (2009) and *The Art of the Pharaohs* (2010), and was coauthor of *Archaeology from Above* (2010) and *The Past Revealed: Great Discoveries in Archaeology* (2010).